Accounting Made Easy

The Evolution of and Need for Basic Understanding of Accounting

Jacob Scott

Table of Contents

Introduction

It is hard to envision how we ended up using numbers to tell stories. It was a matter of necessity but that does not take away the innovation it took to flesh out the numbering system. Think about each group of people coming up with their unique system that would meet their needs independent of other groups of people. It's almost as if we hit a wall that we could not climb without a good grasp of number theory.

When most people talk about accounting they branch off into the mathematics and science and how numbers allowed people to make these grand calculations financially. While that may be true, it is not the inspiration for accounting at all. Accounting practices were inspired by commerce and economics, the need to keep track of what we have and then trade that fairly with others.

If you raise cattle, for example, it is important to know how many cattle you have so that if some were stolen, lost, or sold you would be able to tell. Being able to track the numbers is not the only element. You need some way to communicate the amount of, money, food or tools that you want in exchange for your cattle and record those figures. Beyond that, it would also be good for you to be able to record this transaction so you could reference it in the future.

This was where accounting was born. It was a deep-seated need for the human race to record the amount of belongings they had and how they used those belongings. Today, accounting is more complicated than counting cattle, but it is still built on the same principles that gave birth to it those centuries ago. In this book, we will explore these principles and how you can use them to understand accounting from the ground up.

I know accounting is one of those subjects presented as, difficult, and impossible, I remember my accounting textbook had the words "Accounting is by no means an easy subject," written in ink on the first page. This was the same book my brother had used while he was in school years prior and he had included a note saying that what they were about to get themselves into would not be an easy venture. What if he was wrong though? What if there is an easy way for everyone to understand accounting principles and use accounting reports?

I believe this book will do just that. It will provide a new lens through which to view accounting concepts and make everything clear and easy to understand. We have reached a time where everyone needs to understand financial accounting even those who are not in that field. I have worked with and spoken to so many people who thought accounting was only for the gurus and they did not need to invest in it because it was not their work. The irony was, that the very same people would later come to me with bank statements, budgets, and all forms of accounting reports and ask me to help read them or even create them.

This is what accounting is after all. The science of counting, or accounting, and being accountable as well. If you do not go to work and stay at home taking care of your family, you still need to be accountable for how you use the resources you have in the house and for how you spend your time. If you use money, then you need to plan how you are going to use the money and then need a system that captures the transactions so that you can look back at the usage and use it to make plans for the future. There is a place for accounting in everyone's life.

When you use money or buy anything at all, you are already in on the accounting game. Instead of trying to avoid learning accounting because it's hard, it is best to learn as much as you can and use it as effectively as possible. Now more than ever, there is the need to run our own financial records and accounts. The rise in online business and consumerism means that whether you are selling or buying, you need to be in control of the flow of money and have an understanding of how your resources are being used. The days of tangible transactions are being replaced by digital methods, automatic payments, and subscriptions.

Think of it this way; money, among other resources that you have, are your workers. You can give them different tasks and have them come back at the end of the day or month with a report of what they have done. Now imagine money comes to you and in its report, it only accounts for half the things it did or even less than that. Even worse, imagine money refuses to account for anything. You are left to just guess and think that it was a good job. You cannot even plan for what it will do in the coming weeks and you have no idea whether it will be there.

Would you keep such an employee? Certainly not, but that is what could be happening with your resources right now, if you are not taking the time to account for, and report how you get and use your money, it's as good an employee who does what they wish. Not for long though. Through this interactive guide, I will teach you everything I know about accounting so that by the end you will be able to read any type of accounting report, create accounting entries, and apply the concepts of accounting to your life. It does not matter if you are learning this because you want to start a small business or because you want to just manage your household. The resources in this book will help to achieve all of that.

For you to benefit from this journey, I would like to invite you to be as involved as you can. I will include journal prompts and exercises in the book that you can use to practice the ideas that will be introduced. Before we get started, I would like to invite you to get a journal. If you have an empty one already, that is great. If not, I would advise you to get a physical journal that you can make notes in. There is something about writing things down by hand as you go through thoughts that is very engaging and may help you to understand these concepts better.

Now, if you are ready for the journey, let's go!

Chapter 1:

What is Accounting?

Accounting is storytelling using numbers. It is the practice of comparing what you have at a point in time to what you had when you started. Do you have more now, indicating a profit? Or less, which results in a loss. We will be discussing these terms in more detail throughout this book, since this is the essence of financial accounting.

How often do you communicate with numbers? A lot more often than you might realize. Numbers are an effective language and a powerful way of communication under the right circumstances. In financial circles, the most common is an annual review, such as every calendar year, or at tax time.

The influence of numbers can be seen in how they are used in almost every area of life, be it recording scores in sports, measurements, depicting a person's financial wealth, and even age and time. These are all concepts that we need to understand where we are and where we are going.

Accounting focuses more on financial numbers. It takes advantage of these properties of numbers and uses them to construct reports and statements that can help us understand how we have been using our finances and make decisions to use them better. According to Fernando (2023), "Accounting is the process of recording financial transactions about a business. The accounting process includes summarizing, analyzing, and reporting these transactions to oversight agencies, regulators, and tax collection entities." Essentially, accounting is the ability to interpret what is happening with your money and write about it using numbers. It's the ability to speak the language of numbers and being able to read it.

Now let's look at the very beginning and try to see how the world of accounting has evolved through the years. There have been so many changes to the accounting concepts we use today and understanding how they came to be will give you the perfect base for creating an accounting system that works for you.

Defining Accounting

I know I said that accounting is the ability to understand the use of numbers to tell stories about financial positions and wealth; while that is true, it's only the beginning. There is so much more to accounting. Calculations create the base of accounting. They are the method through which we acquire all the data to structure into the reports that we will then use. They provide more concepts and ideas that make accounting useful to everyone in everyday life. According to Tamplin (2023):

"Accounting is the art of recording, classifying, and summarizing transactions and events. In the first place, we maintain the records of transactions by writing various accounting books like journals and ledgers, etc.

These records are then classified into suitable headings and groups. This classification is important because all information must be seen in a proper perspective to be meaningful.

After the basic records have been suitably classified into groups, the information provided by the groups is summarized into accounting statements (e.g., statements showing the calculation of profit and loss or the business's financial position)." (para. 4)

Think of it this way, the ability to prepare accounting systems is not more important than the ability to read them, In addition to that, you would be better off if you also know how to use that information in real life. Accounting is meant to be useful, to help you make decisions and understand what is happening with your resources, and the impact on your life, and business. Therefore, before you even get into the numbers, you need to know why you are getting into accounting and what benefit you want to gain from it.

If you do not have a good understanding of why you are using accounting principles then you will waste your time. While the reports you create might even be accurate, they will not provide meaningful information to you because you will not have designed them correctly. One of the first things we will think about is why you are learning about accounting. I need you to have an idea of what you are looking for now so that when you get to the sections that answer those questions, you will completely understand what will be happening.

At this point, I want you to turn to your journal and write about why accounting is important to you and what you are looking forward to learning both from it, and about it. I am going to go over a few reasons why people learn accounting and from that, you may want to identify the parts that help to make your life better and incorporate them into your note collection in your journal. Note that this list will not be complete; however, and you should not leave something out just because it's not covered. It is your business, your life, and your financial well-being, do everything you can to understand it and improve it.

Understanding How Businesses Operate Financially

The most important reason for learning accounting concepts is to understand the impact of operations on the businesses. Accounts are the skeleton of the operations of any business. This is because accounts look at how money moves through the entire business to inject life into it. The accounts show how the money moves into the business and how and where it flows out; these pathways are like the veins of the business. If you want to see how your business is performing, then you will need to see the accounting statements However, as previously mentioned it's not just about seeing the accounting statements, it's also about being able to interpret them.

Most large companies publish their accounting statements publicly because they are publicly traded companies. A publicly traded company is a company that sells shares of its ownership to the public. These shares can be bought and sold on stock exchanges, and anyone can own a piece of the company. Publicly traded companies are required to disclose financial information to the public, and they are subject to government regulations.

If you take some time to read these published accounts, you can get a view of what the business is spending most of its money on, how much it is making, and where the money is coming from. This is the beauty of accounting. If you run your own business, you do not have to guess where your money goes and where it comes from, you will be able to see all of that through your accounting statements.

Preparing and Analyzing Financial Statements

Accounting is at the heart of business decision making and for this to be done, you need to have accounting reports to use as data input. Some people study accounting so they can accurately comply with these statements for different businesses. If you want, you can learn to prepare these accounts for yourself and use the results to make business decisions that will help you to keep a healthy financial bottom line Businesses are there to make money more than everything.

To prepare and analyze financial reports officially as an accountant, you will need to be certification from an accredited financial institution that is recognized by the international accounting standard. This can be a long process of hard work and with good justification. There are a lot of laws and regulations around the practice of accounting and therefore you will need to spend a lot of time learning the different accounting standards before you go and work for a big company.

Managing and Reporting on Financial Data

Another reason people want to learn about accounting is to manage financial data correctly and keep it safe. There are also concepts of data management and security when it comes to accounting that you will want to learn about further or to provide accounting services to other companies. We cover most of the nuance ideas around data management and security in future chapters, along with safe guards against cyber attacks as the main threat to accounting online. Again, if this is for other companies, it will be a challenging but very possible learning curve. however, you also need to learn to manage data and security for yourself as well. Because of the way technology has advanced in the past few years, people are now more vulnerable than they have ever been online and unfortunately, most of our financial activity is simultaneously moving to online platforms.

In the past few years, companies have lost a lot of money to hacking. For example, in 2011 it is estimated that companies lost an average of $12.5 billion from hacking schemes alone (Stanescu, 2012). This shows that there is a need for you to know how to manage, monitor, and store your personal financial information online regardless of whether you are a business or not.

Complying With Accounting Regulations

Something we touched on in the previous point is how accounting is such a heavily regulated practice. Accounting statements are used for many functions, including compensation, taxes, and shared price determination. All of these are concepts that involve both the citizens and the government; therefore, authorities need to make sure that all the accounting reports are accurate and complete. This branch of accounting is often called forensic accounting due to the extensive analysis involved.

If you are interested in this branch of accounting, then you will want to become an auditor. An auditor is a person who looks at accounting statements along with other documents and tries to determine if they are accurate and follow the accounting standards they are supposed to. Auditing is like looking at the finished product to make sure there are no defects before it goes out for use. Each company will have its own internal auditors and then the regulating bodies will also have their auditors that will verify the accounting statements of the company.

Making Sound Financial Decisions

The most common reason for learning accounting is so that you can be able to make good financial decisions for your business, your life, and personal wealth. How many times have you looked back at how you spent your money or invested it and wished you could turn back the hand of time and change your decisions? Quite often I would imagine.

This point demonstrates how informative accounting can be. While most people leave the idea of accounting to huge corporations that have to make multi-million dollar decisions, it's just as effective for everyday life and everyday decision-making. If you are an accountant by profession or someone who knows a bit about accounting, then you will develop a logical, problem solving way of thinking that will help you resolve issues in everyday life. Think about it this way; accounting is a layered and organized system of thought that progresses all the way from income to output.

The advantage of accounting is that once you manage data collection for finances, you will also collect all sorts of data and observe your environment. This will lead to preparing and analyzing the data with due care and eventually making better quality decisions in life. So accounting will not only help you to have a profitable financial life, but it will also help you in all the other areas of your life.

Investing Money Wisely

The next reason for learning accounting is so you can make wiser investments with your money. An investment is when you put your money toward a business or endeavor that is meant to give your money back with added value. It focuses on potential growth. It can be difficult to pick out which business or product to invest in. One of the methods people use is to look at the financial success of a company.

The unfortunate part is, that it is not as easy as it might seem to identify which companies are doing well and which companies are not. Let me give you an example that you can use to conceptualize this problem. Assume there are three companies; Company D, Company F, and Company K. The first one, Company D, has been in operation for 10 years and has grown six-fold since it was started reaching a total value of 23 million dollars. It has made a total of one million in profit over the years.

Company F on the other hand, has grown 54% since it was opened 9 years ago and is currently worth $400,000 and has made a total profit of 1 million. Lastly, Company K has only been operating for half a year and is worth 25 million dollars with no recorded profits so far.

Which company do you think would be the best option to invest in? Do you have enough information in the above statements, or are there other factors that would help you decide? You will see that it is not as easy as looking at the size of the company or the annual profits and then making a decision. There are many other things that you need to think about that were not mentioned in the scenario. We will be looking at these other factors later in the book. This means if you are going to make the best decisions, you need to have a good idea of accounting reports, the impact, and what they mean.

Starting Your Own Business

There has been a surge in the number of people willing to learn accounting over the last few years. This increase correlates with the increase in online businesses, demonstrating that as more and more people start getting into business, they start looking to learn to manage their businesses. If you are also starting your own business, then this book will help you to grow your knowledge to manage your business better.

When you are running a small business, it might be too expensive to hire an accountant, and for this reason, most people end up learning to handle their own accounting books. The process of managing your accounting books is not easy, but its benefits will pay off. One of the things you can expect to happen is that you will have a good understanding of what is going on in your business as it grows.

Fortunately, there are also a couple of tools that you can use to help you with your bookkeeping, making your learning curve easier to navigate. Later in Chapter 9, we will go over some digital tools that you can learn from and use to manage your personal and small business's financial needs.

When you only see the financial statements at the end of the week or the month, you are getting your business status at that point, often missing how the business flourished throughout the period when the data was collected. If you manage your books, however, you will be able to see which days had the high sales and when you had the unexpected expenses among other things. This means you will be able to make better decisions for your business and thrive in the end.

Whatever your reasons for learning accounting, you are in the right place. Accounting is such a beautiful system of storytelling that I am sure you will enjoy learning the principles. When we started this section I asked you to determine your reasons for learning about accounting and record them in your journal. I hope some of these prompts have helped you to do exactly that. If what you want is not among what we have listed, it's okay, there are many other reasons for learning accounting that we did not cover.

Now you know why you want to learn accounting, let's look at the different types of accounting, how they work together, and how they can be integrated into your life. As we go through this book remember that you are in charge of your learning experience. The more you engage and take time to think about how these concepts work in your life, the more you will see improvements in your financial life.

Accounting will affect some of the most important parts of your life and business, such as costs , profit and loss, debts, property acquisition and sale, planning, and ruling processes within business and finance. These are issues you do not want to leave to chance and should actively monitor.

The Role of an Accountant

Accountants play a vital role in the successful preparation and presentation of accounts for any business. They are responsible for keeping track of financial transactions, preparing financial statements, and ensuring that the company complies with financial regulations pursuant to the type of company and the location. The role of an accountant will go beyond this now and then depending on the needs of the organization but these are the main duties.

The accountant is the financial storyteller, collecting data on what is happening in the business and then compiling it to tell a story that everyone else can read easily and understand. Accounting involves hundreds of transactions between the company and its stakeholders; so many transactions that no one would be able to make sense of them if they were all presented at the same time. We need accountants to make the data make sense for everyone else in the company.

Accountants also provide financial analysis and advice to help businesses make sound financial decisions through consultancy services. It can be very hard to manage even the most simplified statements and hiring an accountant for consultancy is one way to make sure you fully understand what is happening with the business financially, especially if you don't have a full-time accountant on staff. Let's look at some of the specific tasks for accountants and how you might use these services to improve your business.

Keep Track of Financial Transactions

The first, and probably one of the most important parts of the accounting process is keeping track of every transaction that takes place within the business. Accounting is data interpretation for the most part, therefore, the accountant needs to make sure the data is recorded accurately before they start to process the information. A business will have a lot of different transactions each month, including all the income and expenses, as well as tracking assets and liabilities.

You can follow the same process with your finances as the first step to managing and improving your financial health. The main idea is that everything that happens should be recorded somewhere; be it a journal or a digital application that allows the capture of every transaction as it happens. For starters, consider recording everything that happens without categorizing the data, just add all activities in one place grouping by the date it occurred. This is a good introduction to accounting as it helps you to get the feel of keeping and managing your records.

Just recording everything alone should allow you to improve your understanding of your cash flow if done habitually and consistently. Our minds are not very good at remembering activities that just happen throughout the month, but if we take the time to write these events down, we will remember them and have a better picture of how we make and spend money.

Prepare Financial Statements

After receiving the information and making sure they record it accurately and correctly, the accountants have to group the information and create financial statements. Using the data received, the accountant will be able to separate the data into different groups so that it can be used for different types of accounting statements. They need to know how to classify all of the transactions so that the statement is an accurate summary of what happened throughout the month. For example, if over a hundred payments are made for a subscription to a service that the business offers, the accounting statements would then show just the total paid and not all of the individual payments.

It is the role of an accountant to prepare financial accounting statements that capture transactions for the company through thorough summaries of the company's financial activities. The most common types of statements accountants prepare include:

- income statement

- balance sheet

- cash flow statement

We will cover these statements in more detail in a later chapter.

You can also adopt these ideas for your personal finances and use them to record and interpret your own transactions. To make this process easier, I would advise that you use a digital platform that will allow you to record the transactions under various categories. These digital applications will also have the function of giving you summarized results from the data you have shared. Having statements for your financial activity should not be a function for your business only. This is something that you should get in the habit of doing to have control over your financial well-being.

Analyze Financial Statements

As we mentioned before, the financial statements themselves might become irrelevant if the person who is looking at them has no idea what they mean. In the second step, the accountant will do their best to make sure that the accounting statements are as clear as possible, difficulty understanding the accounts. You can also have the accountant analyze the accounts and help you to understand what the numbers mean. If the accounting statements are the stories told in numbers, the accountant can be viewed as the interpreter of that language as well.

This is one of the main reasons to go for accounting consultancy next to credit management. Accountants use their knowledge of accounting principles and financial analysis to interpret financial statements and identify trends that exist within the statements. This information can be used to help businesses make sound financial decisions in the future.

In the same way, you can have your accounts well documented and well presented, but it is helpful to have other people help with a fresh look at the accounts and give their opinion.

Advise Businesses on Financial Matters

Accountants will be able to understand the impact of decisions made on the financial statements already there. For example, a big company has been running for a long time and they have been growing very slowly while expanding their business.

Lately; however, the company has decided to start selling shares on the public stock market and they want to know if the inflow of cash will help with anything and how they should price their shares. Getting an accountant to look at their books can help them to see what arrears they can work on in their operations to save money and cut down costs so that they use their equity more effectively. In addition to this, the accountant may also evaluate the accounts and advise on a fair price for the shares or alternative ways of funding the business.

The world of accounting affects almost every part of your life. Anything that gives you money or that you use money for is an accounting issue. This being said, you can also book a session with an accountant for a consultation when you have decisions to make. If you want to do something big like starting a business or buying a house or car, you can get recommendations and advice to finance the project among other things. If you have looked at your accounts but still do not understand what is happening, then there is no shame in looking for help from an accounting professional.

Some of the things that an accountant can provide advice for include tax planning, investment strategies, and risk management. All of these are important areas of life that you need to manage at all times. Or you can have your accountant do it for you.

Comply With Financial Regulations

There is one more service that accountants offer simultaneously. Accountants are responsible for ensuring that their clients comply with all applicable financial regulations for the type of business and the work that has to be done. Accountants have an obligation to their clients according to their certification and duty to be ethical and compliant in all the advice they give. This is why most accounting firms will have harsh punishments against things like fraud, and tax evasion attempts. These ruin the reputation of the accountants, the institutions that certify them, and the companies that they work for.

Keeping the books of a company is a timely and costly task but one that is necessary to avoid heavy penalties and fines. For businesses, reputation is important and they will do everything they can to maintain high standards, making accounting important for every business regardless of niche or size.

It's important to understand that accounting principles before you can become a part of it. There are so many aspects to being an accountant that make it one of the most diverse professions ever. At the core, however, is the central idea; determining a way to capture and present financial truths easily for decision-making.

Now, let's move on to the next chapter and look at what it means to be an accountant, taking a glimpse beneath the calculators and stereotypes that come with the title. Just like accounting itself, being an accountant is a rich and exciting endeavor. You will see this as you delve further into this book.

Chapter 2:

Not Just a Math Wiz; Skills an

Accountant Needs

When I worked in the human resources field for a huge corporation, one of my friends were Obert from accounting, and Martha from regulatory affairs. We spent most of the breaks and lunch times together talking about work Whenever we were together and a calculation had to be made, instead of pulling out the phone to calculate, everyone would look at Obert and expect him to know the answer off the top of his head.

Obert would always look at us in disapproval and retort, "I am not a mathematician, I am an accountant. You guys know those are not the same thing, right?" We did not know that then, but I do now, after working on so many projects and running a few businesses myself. I finally see accounting for what it is. Behind all het stereotypical nonsense about numbers, accounting is so much more.

What's more, I am a horrible mathematician but have grown to become a very impressive accountant. I have a good understanding of how to manage and present financial ideas, budgets, and everything in between. The accounting system is such that—if you set it up right—you will not need to be proficient with numbers to maintain and run a good accounting system. In this chapter, I will show you some of the other skills that you will need to become a good accountant, and shocking as it may be, being good at mathematics is less than 10% of the skills you will need.

There has been a rise in the importance of soft skills for successful accountants, particularly in the recruitment process, where crucial skills amongst the best-in-class talent are assessed (Morris, 2022). So, what are soft skills in the workplace and why are they important? Let's dive in and see if we can answer this question.

Technical Knowledge

Accounting is a subject of principles, which means it is guided by rules that determine what can be done with which type of entries. It is more important to know how to use the numbers instead of how to calculate the number. For instance, if you get $49 from a friend to start a business and then you use $24 to start a business which makes you $25 by the end of the month. How do you find the profit for the month?

It would seem straight forward. You take the money you received and then compare it to what you have by the end of the day. But wait, there are so many answers even with that approach. For instance, do you just say since you made $25 from $49 then you have a loss? Maybe you can say you make about 50% profit since $25 is almost half of $49. But that does not seem right either. In fact, which amount is the investment, the $49 you received, or the $24 you used?

This is a very simple example to show that it is not the actual calculation itself that will be your problem most cases. It is going to be something far greater; the governing principles. This is the number one skill any accountant needs to have. You need to know what the principals are and how they work in different situations. If you fail to do this, you can throw off your accounting records and sadly that would not be the end of it. Remember that accounting records are also the reference point for decision-making and management. Having incorrect accounting reports will lead to incorrect decisions, and the entire boniness could be at risk because of it.

We have already gone over the main principles in accounting and how they work together to create the accounting reports that you will then use in the end for management and decision-making. The principles that we went over are only the beginning of accounting practice. It is dynamic and will change depending on the organization, the current economy and business plans. This brings us back to the silver principle. Accounting is personal. It's meant to tell the story of your business, and that story will be differently from other stories. While all businesses have the same general guiding principles, they are all unique in their plans and goals and cannot be presented as the same thing.

Technical knowledge includes knowledge of accounting procedures as well as financial applications. There are so many procedures that go into creating the accounting statements that can be used by the business to make decisions and plan for the future. It takes an accountant a few years to know how to execute these procedures accurately and how to interpret the outcome of the processes.

As an accountant, you will be expected to know how to calculate different elements like tax, profit margins, and cost ratios among many others. This takes focus and dedication, but can be acquired through training and practice.

In addition to the procedures, you will also need to know what the tools are and how to use them. Most of the tools used for accounting are digital with the majority being online and cloud tools. The software used for accounting is very specific and basic budgeting templates can be found through tools such as Excel. Over time, the tools for accounting have become more and more accessible to everyone. We will look at the tools and software used for accounting in detail in a future chapter, but you should know that accounting heavily relies on the use of computers and other devices along with different software.

Creativity and Analytical Thinking

Accounting is about being smart with numbers; being able to tell a story from a collection of numbers that would otherwise mean nothing. This system is protected f guidelines and regulations that determine how the accounts are prepared ensuring consistency and accuracy. Because of this, most people think accounting is another rigid task that you can do as long as you know the rules but one that does not require any creativity or analytical thinking.

In actuality, accounting is one of the most creative ventures in the world. It might have its limitations on what w it is done and who can do it, but it requires an open and intelligent mind to understand and synergize the different aspects of the subject. The thing with accounting is there is going to be a transaction that you have never seen before, something that requires you to not only use the standards and regulations but also use your analytical skills to find the best way to capture and convey the information.

Creativity, after all, is about finding the most unique solutions to the problems that we face. Accounting is all about finding solutions to different problems while still making sure that the solutions you come up with will be in line with the guidelines and regulations. This makes it not only a creative or analytical venture, but a great combination of the two. It's the perfect balance between openness and order. It is not easy balancing these two.

Some statements are prepared specifically to recognize problems and address them. You need the ability to identify, analyze, and evaluate information, and to make sound judgments based on that information. All of this will depend on your creativity and your analytical skills.

Communication Skills and Leadership Abilities

I had a conversation with a colleague one time who was working in human resources but wanted to move from there into accounting. One of the arguments they gave was that they just wanted to work behind a desk and not have to interact with people a whole lot. To them, accounting was their way of getting a job where all they did was run numbers behind a screen all day and never have to interact with anyone. However, anyone who has been in accounting knows that this could not be further from the truth.

An accountant is not only a leader but they are also required to have strong interpersonal skills through and through. Okay, let's go back to the main duties of an accountant and consider if it's even possible to stay away from people as an accountant. A good start might be looking at things like consultancy and presenting financial statements. Accountants are storytellers, and you tell stories to people and need to be able to hear them out as well to be effective.

When you are an accountant, you will need to be able to explain the financial statements to business leaders and do it clearly. Because you will be responsible for updating and maintaining the financial records of the company, you need to make sure that all the departments that receive products and services record these transactions accurately. Accounting is the one of the departments that has to work with everyone all the time. It might be discussing the cost of raw materials with production, payroll with human resources, cost efficiency with operations, or even credits and debts with sales. Accounting has to make sure all the financial transactions are in line with the guidelines of the company and the regulating bodies.

Remember Obert from accounting, the accountant I used to work with? When he joined the company, he was really quiet and kept to himself quite a bit. However, after a few years of managing the budgets, running payments, and having to negotiate with other employees, he became a leader who would communicate and ensure the use of the responsible use of resources. I will admit, I was one of the people who would reach out to him every time there was an issue with a payment and I needed to learn how to navigate it. To be honest, now that I think about it. Obert's influence was one of the reasons I ended up becoming interested in accounting and eventually put all my knowledge in this book.

As a leader, an accountant must be able to provide clear direction, motivate, and inspire their team, and hold them accountable for their use of allocated finances. There is a responsibility to manage the second most important resource for the company—its money—and to make sure all transactions are in line with the guiding principles of the regulating bodies.

Great communication skills help build relationships with clients and colleagues. When you are in accounting, you depend on data that is often collected by the other departments. This means having a good relationship with your colleagues can help you to get your work done more effectively. When discussing profit and loss criteria or reports with clients, being able to adjust the level of communication to the audience is key. For example, it would be an asset to use visual aids and charts to represent the figures when necessary.

This is the same with your clients. You should be able to have conversations with your clients even when you are not talking about work. This will make it easier to talk to them when you are making presentations or trying to explain something in the accounts to them. While accounting is not hard, it is very complex and needs to be explained with great care. You will meet people who will have a really hard time understanding what you present and explain, so you need to have the flexibility to meet their level and explain in a way that they can understand. When discussing profit and loss criteria or reports with clients, being able to adjust the level of communication to the audience is key. For example, it would be an asset to use visual aids and charts to represent the figures when necessary.

Being an accountant is complex, challenging, fun, and exciting at the same time. It's not just about the regulations and procedures. It's not even just about the money and the statements; it's about all of that and more. It's in the way you communicate with the clients and colleagues, the way you handle the data and the way you carry yourself and your integrity.

While an accountant will have so much to do, it also depends on the type of accounting they are doing. There are quite a few branches of accounting. In the next chapter, we will explain the different accounting types and how they are used. This section will provide an understanding of accounting and its diversity.

Chapter 3:

Branches of Accounting

You can think of accounting branches in the same way you think of story genres. Each branch focuses on delivering a specific message to a specific audience. The economic world is so diverse you cannot use the same tools for everything; therefore, you need special guiding principles for each branch of accounting. Think of it this way; if you have a business and you are budgeting for the business's expenses, you do not use the same thinking pattern that you would otherwise use for your personal budget.

The differences between the branches of accounting, however, are even more different than your personal life and small business finances might be. This is because each type of business also has its governing laws and regulations, making the accounting terms and processes different. A good example is how a church does not declare profit no matter how much money they have, and therefore does not pay tax in many regions. On the other hand, a corporate business must declare either a profit or a loss and pay tax depending on how much has been made.

It is imperative that you understand which category your needs fall under. By having a clear picture of what type of accounting you need to focus on you can then direct your learning efforts to maximize the knowledge that will affect your finances. Let's discuss some of the most popular branches of accounting and see which ones fit your needs.

Financial Accounting

This is the branch of accounting that is concerned with the preparation of financial statements for external users, such as investors, creditors, and regulators. This is the most popular type of accounting as well, and is the type most accountants working for businesses and corporations use. Because of the regulations on these businesses and the need to communicate the performance of the business, the statements have to be accurate and reflect how the business is doing.

Berry-Johnson (2019), defines financial accounting as:

> Financial accounting is the process of recording, summarizing, and reporting a company's business transactions through financial statements. These statements are (1) the income statement, (2) the balance sheet, (3) the cash flow statement, and (4) the statement of retained earnings. (para. 1)

In a later section, we will go through all of these financial books one by one so you can get a better understanding of what financial accounting is.

Financial accounting is considered in the public interest in most cases, which means the accounts for publicly traded companies must be accessible to the public. Financial accounting can only be done by a certified accountant, at least at the level of big businesses and corporations. The related financial statements provide information about the company's financial position, results of operations, and cash flows.

The company's financial position will often be a reflection of how much money the company has and how much it can use. This provides a glimpse at the health of the company at the time the account is prepared. Investors use this information to decide if they should stay in the company or if they should pull out and find other businesses to invest in.

These accounts focus on the results of the operations at a specific point in time. It might not be fair to judge the position of a company by the amount of money made or the liquidity it has when the statements are prepared. It is usually best to look at what the results from the operations have been, and the projections, which can help to give a better picture of the company's financial health. If a construction company has been working for a year , for example, and has not made any profit in that time, but has completed more stages in the project for less money than planned to that point, then it has done very well.

Lastly, but equally as important, the financial statements will also show the cash flow of the company for the period in question. This is the story of how much money was received by the company and where it was allocated. Investors will often want to know what the company is using the income for and the cash flow statements will show the investors just that.

Another stakeholder interested in these type of accounts are creditors, who use financial statements to assess a company's creditworthiness. Often, a creditor will ask a company to submit some of their recent account statements to prove that they can repay the loan before they agree to the terms. This is also common practice with big purchases like land, buildings, and factories where the buying company might be asked to provide copies of their accounting statements to make sure that they are liquid enough to pay for the purchase.

Regulators use the financial statements to ensure that companies are complying with financial regulations. Because companies have to pay for tax among other statutory invoices, the regulating bodies will check and use the financial accounts to determine the amount that you need to pay under these statutory requirements.

Being the most popular branch of accounting, financial accounting is a complex and demanding field, but it is also a very rewarding one. Financial accountants play a vital role in the financial world, and they are essential to the success of businesses of all sizes.

Financial accounting is governed by generally accepted accounting principles (GAAP), which are a set of rules that companies must follow when preparing their financial statements. In addition, there are international standards, national regulations, and internal guidelines. All of these will create a template that helps the company to create the most accurate and consistent throughout.

These transactions do not end here though. Financial accounting is also subject to auditing, which is a process of reviewing financial statements to ensure that they are accurate, compliant, and complete. We will look at auditing in this chapter as a separate branch of accounting as it often is.

In a nutshell, financial accounting is an important process through which the accountant captures, stores, processes, and presents the financial transactions of the company for a given period. These accounts are what businesses then use for decision-making and also what the investors use to understand the health of the business.

Managerial Accounting

Accounting is a language that some people within the company struggle to understand. To tell these people the story of the company's performance, you will need to change the language to something that everyone will understand. The most important internal group that needs to know what the financial statements are saying is the management team. Because of this, there is a branch of accounting that aims to teach managers how to interpret and use accounting reports.

Managerial accounting provides financial and non-financial information to managers within a company. Imagine you are the operations manager for a company, and while you understand how to hire and train the employees for the job, you might not know how to cost the labor appropriately or how to match the cost of the labor to the operations. It becomes important therefore to bring the accounting concepts to the manager so that they can make financial considerations as they make the major decisions.

There are many other reasons managers should understand accounting functions, including: being able to properly set processes for the company's goods and services, allocating resources across departments, and properly measuring performance. This makes managerial accounting different for each department and manager. Despite that, the basic principles and accounting statements must be understood by everyone.

The main difference between managerial accounting and financial accounting is that it is not used to provide information to external users like investors or creditors. Instead, it is used to provide information that will only be used by the managers and employees to monitor the progress of the business and make sure it keeps going. Accounting has two outputs, the information that is provided to the external stakeholders so that they know what is happening with the business, and the information provided internally so that the management and employees can find ways to improve the operations of the company.

Let's explore how the information provided for management is going to be used by the company to make decisions for the business. The first reason, and one of the most important, is to set prices for the products and services that the business provides. Every business is running to make a profit. To do this, they must make more money than they use for creating the goods they sell or providing the services they have.

However, it is not always that easy to determine how much it costs to make the products and sell them. There is so much that goes into sourcing the resources needed for a product or service Because of this, the business may fail to calculate the actual cost of acquiring materials, manufacturing and selling the products and services. This will affect the prices you set for the retail of the goods and services. Managers use the reports prepared for them to identify how much the company is spending on production and distribution, then decide on a price that will cover all the costs and make a profit. In some cases the decision might not even be to make a profit. Some strategic decisions for market penetration might have managers choose to break even or take a certain percentage of losses temporarily. This would not be possible if they do not understand what the actual cost of producing the goods and providing the services is, based on the accounting statements.

Beyond the costing aspect, one of the most important tasks that the management team has is resource allocation. Because a company can have so many departments with different activities that need money, the managers have to decide how much will be given to which department and when. This does not only apply to money. The managers have to decide how much labor is required for each of the departments along with the equipment needed there as well.

Ultimately, the departments that have a bigger contribution to the bottom line of the business will get first preference when it comes to resources so that the business can make more products and more money. The supporting departments will also need to get enough resources to keep the business going, but when constrained, it is prudent for the business to make sure the core activities keep going so they do not lose revenue or fail to provide the goods and services to the market.

Managerial accounts are also used to measure performance through key performance indicators (KPIs). Businesses use managerial accounting information to measure the performance of specific criteria among the different divisions of the company. It is possible to measure the output of each individual or department using the number of units produced, target dates met, or the quality of work done. This is combined with the compensation scheme to make sure the employees are getting paid their full worth.

Beyond the employees, KPIs can also measure the performance of different branches of the company in different locations. Looking at the costs by location or division and comparing that to output and profits, the management team can determine which locations are successful and learn from them to take what they are doing well and bring it to the rest of the organization.

My personal favorite is how you will be able to evaluate investment opportunities using the managerial accounts. In most cases, managerial accounts will also include comparisons of the performance in the market, an analysis of projected costs, and an analysis of the opportunities that are available in the industry. Managers can use the accounting reports to find new ventures to steer the company investments toward. Before looking at investing in other markets, managers will also look at other things like whether they should move to a new location, if they need new equipment, and whether they should expand the business.

Receiving and understanding managerial financial reports provides the ability to plan for the future. When you have a good understanding of the past, the present, and the projections for the future—which is what is offered by managerial accounting—then you are good to hit the ground running and create the future you want for your business.

This information allows managers to make budgets and forecasts that can mitigate any risks before they even come about. This is one of the big uses of accounting actually; to help management see the financial future of the company and do something about it before it is too late to avert the risk.

Auditing

The accuracy of your accounting statements is imperative, so there is a separate accounting depart that is there to double-check and make sure the accounts are accurate and that the processes are being recorded correctly. Auditing is like the policing part of accounting. Its job is to review and verify financial statements and other records to ensure accuracy and compliance with laws and regulations.

My first experience with auditing was when I had a roommate after getting my first job. After a few months, I was talking to my roommate, who, as it turned out, was an accountant. I told them I had trouble keeping track of my money and never really knew where the money was going. They asked if I would be okay with them auditing my accounts for free. I agreed and wrote down all my transactions like I had been asked to do.

They looked at the records I had made and started asking me questions about the transactions including things like how I had used the change from certain transactions and where I was keeping the money. It did not take me long to realize that auditing was a very difficult process to go through and one that would poke holes in every mistake you have in your process. This was great because it prepared me for the large-scale audits that I would later go through at work.

It's important to note that auditing is not only for the accounting department, but everyone and every department. Since it's a check to see if everything is being done well, it definitely can be used in all departments. If you only check your accounting department, then you might miss some processes that are incorrect. For example, if the employees are being underpaid or if the supply chain has some fraudulent activity with supplier selection. So an audit checks everything in the company to make sure there is alignment throughout. This is also be true for your personal life. You can not only audit your financial transactions, but everything else in your life.

Auditors are often independent professionals hired to provide an objective opinion on the financial statements of a company or organization, but all companies must also have internal audits where they have their auditors check if they are in keeping with the standards and regulations.

The goal of auditing is to assure investors, creditors, government entities, and other stakeholders that the financial statements are accurate and that the company is operating in compliance with laws and regulations. Any betrayal of this trust could seriously damage the reputation of the company while attracting investigations by the government and other regulatory bodies.

Let's discuss the main responsibilities of an auditor and show you how you can apply these to your own life.

Responsibilities of an Auditor

The first thing an auditor has to do is review the financial statements of the company. As they check the statements, they are scanning for areas that might have been miscalculated or where errors might have occurred. This process is not only done for the financial statements that the company shares with the public, but it stretches to all internal reports as well. This includes the accounting reports that are used to determine things like the tax and statutory obligations of the company.

In addition to this, the auditor also inspects the storing and labeling of the company's records. One of the requirements of accounting is that all information be stored in a safe and orderly way. This is to say only the right person should have access to the information when they need it but they should be able to access it easily when needed as well. Auditors will often do checks where they look at the information storage, including how it is stored and even check where the servers are stored and how secure they are if it is a digital accounting system.

On the importance of how accounting records are stored, Grahams (2020), said, "Financial records are the most crucial documents for any startup or enterprise. Securing them has to be the number one goal." I share the same sentiment. These accounting reports and data are your company's biggest secret and you want to make sure that you keep them as safe as you can. This crosses over to your personal life as well, where you should also keep all the major financial decisions to yourself.

While accountants and auditors often work with objective data, sometimes they have to get the opinions and input of management and other employees to create context for the data. This is often done when auditors look at the records and then interview the manager or employee in charge to get more clarity on the processes and procedures that lead to the production of the final product.

This can be a very helpful process for the company, highlighting the main flaws in the operations and guidelines that the company is following. In some cases, the accounts and other records might be misleading but only because of the process of storing, processing, or even capturing the data. The auditors must check that the employees handling the data are trained to do so and that they understand what they are doing.

After making sure that the data is accurate and the processes used to obtain and store it are also compliant, the auditing team will seek approval on the data and processes from the company and the stakeholders. From here, the accountant and analysts can then use the data to make decisions and predictions knowing that the reports they are using are correct and approved.

Based on their findings, auditors will issue an opinion on the financial statements. The opinion can be either a clean opinion, which means that the auditor believes that the financial statements are accurate and that the company is operating in compliance with laws and regulations, or an adverse opinion, which means that the auditor believes that the financial statements are not accurate or that the company is not operating in compliance with laws and regulations.

Auditing is an important process that helps to ensure the accuracy and reliability of financial information as it also helps to protect investors, creditors, and other stakeholders from fraud and other financial reporting errors.

Cost Accounting

Everything in life will cost something, and for businesses, the cost is such an important factor. This is why there is a branch of accounting dedicated to analyzing, understanding, and reducing costs. Because there is so much happening with a business, it can be hard to see where they are incurring expenses and that is where the expert comes in.

Take a big company with seven factories across the country making seven different products. If these products are all distributed differently and manufactured differently, then they will each have different cost structures. Now to add to that, the company will still have operation costs, and distribution and sales costs to get the product to the right market. It can be hard to see where all the money is going unless there is a proper analysis of the costs in the company.

The first step in cost accounting is to manage the creation and approval of budgets. Budgets for the company show how much the company plans on spending and on what. At this stage, the procurement team along with the accounting team can help each other to decide which of the available supplies can provide the services best and at what cost. If the budget is off, then it will be hard for the company to manage the costs as they go along.

After the budget has been created, the finance team will now need to monitor the budget and make sure it is being followed. Because the economic environment is volatile, there will be fluctuations in prices and new costs that the companies could not have foreseen before making the budget. Part of proper cost management is to include contingency funds so that the company can still meet its objectives regardless of these unexpected costs.

Following this, the cost management and accounting team will need to look at the data they have from the period and determined a way to reduce the costs for the next period. There are a lot of considerations that go into cost management and sometimes it might mean getting a very expensive piece of equipment that will cost a lot at purchase but then reduce the costs of production in the long run.

Cost accountants have to then go and present their findings to the management team who will help in making the decisions using the data from the accounts. This is one of the most crucial exercises for any company, definitely something you should do in your life as well.

As we said earlier, accounting management is not only for big companies and corporates, it's for individuals and small businesses as well. Try keeping an eye on your accounts for just one month and see how this would change your financial health. The first step, just like it is for the companies, would be to make a budget. We will go in-depth on how you make a budget that works for you in a later chapter, but for now, we will look at how you can manage costs overall.

When you have your budget, guard it jealously. Your budget is your money, and if you do not take good care of it, you can easily lose it. If you buy things that you were not planning to buy, you will end up failing to buy what you wanted.

I bet when we mentioned how accounting was diverse and varied in the first chapter, you did not think it was to this extent. Accounting can look very different depending on who you are doing it for and why. While we will focus primarily on personal and commercial accounting principles and ideas in this book, it can also be fun to explore the other types of accounting and seek to understand how they vary from accounting for businesses. One area we will always bring into the discussion, is personal accounting. I am a strong believer that your accounting skills are only useful if they apply to your life first.

If you want to learn to handle the finances of a huge company, learn to handle your finances first. It will then become easier for you to bring the skill you have already sharpened in your personal life to the trade. Now that you know what being an accountant is like and what the different types of accounting are, let's take a moment to think about how you are already a part of this ecosystem. Which of the accountant skills do you have, and which one do you need to develop? What type of accounting are you doing and what type do you need to start doing? Take your journal and document your thoughts on this. This will help you to get a clear picture of what you need to focus on.

Next, let's explore some of the basic principles of accounting. In the next chapter, we are going to look at what the basic principles of accounting are using some numbers to make it clearer for you. It's time to grab your calculator and follow along.

Chapter 4:

Basic Principles of Accounting

In accounting, there are guiding concepts that help to keep everything framed, commonly referred to as accounting principles. These principles are the basic guidelines to help create a coherent and globally acceptable understanding of accounting; one that you can understand as well.

In this chapter, we will go over six of the most common accounting principles and see how you can apply them to your personal life and your small business. Remember, accounting is not only about big corporations and huge accounting systems. It can be applied at every stage and for any activity. I want you to grab your journal as we dive into another chapter and jot down the ideas that stand out to you the most.

Be sure to practice these principles as much as you can in your day-to-day life. It might even be for issues that do not necessarily concern money, such as the way you treat your energy and your time. This is why understanding how money works can also help you be more efficient in many other areas of your life.

Double Entry System

The most important principle in accounting is the double entry system, which is the accounting equivalent of the saying "there are always two sides to every story." This principle suggests that every entry should be made twice so that you capture the dual effects of the transaction. If you buy a car for $5,000, two things are happening at the same time. First, you are getting a $5,000 asset and second, you are using $5,000 of your cash.

Every transaction is recorded once as a debit and then once as a credit to make for the double entry. You need to credit the giver and debit the receiver. If you do this, the accounting books will end up balanced and more accurate. Following up with our example, if you have $25,000 and you buy the car for $5,000 but only record receiving a new asset for $5,000 without debiting the $5,000 cash, at the end of the accounting period you will have $5,000 more on your statement than you will have in reality.

The double entry system is based on the accounting equation, which states that assets = liabilities + equity. In accounting, assets are resources that a company owns and expects to benefit from in the future. These are often classified into two groups; tangible, such as cash, equipment, buildings, vehicles, or inventory, and intangible assets, such as patents, trademarks, goodwill, and bonds among others. Assets are important because they provide a company with the resources it needs to operate and generate revenue. They have the same effect in your personal life as well. While some assets might not be helping you to get money, they will provide some value that will make your quality of life better.

On the other side of the equation, we have liabilities which are debts or obligations that a company owes to its creditors. They are claims against the company's assets that must be paid in the future. Liabilities can be classified as either current liabilities—those due within a year—or long-term liabilities which can be paid back after over time. There are many types of liabilities, but the most common are accounts payable, notes payable, accrued expenses, income taxes payable, and long-term debt.

In your personal life, this will include things like your mortgage, loans credit card debt that you have to pay off. You should keep a very sharp eye on your liabilities because they can easily get out of hand and lead to unfavorable financial situations. If you have more liability that you can manage, you may eventually have to declare bankruptcy and lose your assets in an attempt to pay your outstanding debt. This is the main reason companies close actually. You would think the biggest measure of whether a company is doing well is if it makes a profit or not, but not always. Sometimes, having too many liabilities can lead to a business closing even if they are recording profits every year.

Here, we are introduced to the idea of equity. Equity is the difference between your assets and liabilities. This means if you look at the total value of the items you own and remove all the money you need to pay back, then you will get the value for your equity. Because of this, it is also known as shareholders' equity or net worth. This figure represents how much the business has as profit, the amount that would be paid out to the investors if the company were to shut down and liquidate. The first thing that will happen when a company closes is the liquidation of assets to pay all of the liabilities and only the remaining value is for the owners of the company.

Let's go back to one of the reasons for learning accounting; making wise financial decisions. Imagine the following were two companies' balance sheets:

Company K: Assets $5,700,000 = liabilities $4,900,000 + equity $800,000.

Company W: Assets $3,000,000 = liabilities $1,500,000 + equity $1,500,000.

Looking at the two companies above, which one would you invest in if the shares for both had the same price? While it might seem like a good idea to invest in a bigger company all the time, take some time to consider each of the parts of the equation and what they mean, and then make your decision based on that. Use your journal to write down what you think would be the best way forward and why. We will cover the balance sheet in depth in a later chapter, but you will need to understand the basics of this formula for the rest of the book to make sense to you.

All the resources that a company owns and expects to benefit from are referred to as assets. If you have a T-shirt making business, then your assets include:

- a heat press machine

- sewing machine

- building and store front

- vehicle for order deliveries

- Intellectual capital

Most assets are things you can touch, like cash, inventory, and property, but sometimes assets can be intangible. Examples of intangible assets include things like patents, trademarks, intellectual capital, and goodwill, which all add value to the business and can be recorded in the financial reports of the business but are not tangible. Assets are important because they represent the value of a company's resources, a concept we will go over in depth when we discuss how to run accounts for your small business in a later chapter. As we have already seen from the balance sheet equation, the assets are a very important element in calculating the value of the company.

Equity can be increased and controlled through the issuing of new shares, retaining earnings, limiting liabilities or by selling assets. It can be controlled by paying dividends, issuing debt, or incurring losses in the period in question. Shares are the stake that each investor or shareholder has in the company, often a percentage of the equity of the company. For instance, if a company issued 5,000 shares and you have 100 of the shares, then you would be entitled to 2% of the company's equity.

The balance sheet equation must always be true, so if a company makes a purchase, the transaction must be recorded in such a way that the accounting equation remains in balance. For example, if a company purchases $5,000 worth of inventory, the transaction would be recorded as follows:

Credit: Inventory $5,000

Debit: Accounts payable $5,000

This transaction increases the company's inventory asset by $5,000 and increases its accounts payable liability by the same amount. So every time you buy an asset, you have to affect either your equity or your liabilities at the same time while fulfilling the principal in full. You cannot take without giving. The double entry system is complex, but it is essential for accurate and reliable financial reporting as it guarantees balance throughout the accounting and reporting process. This is such a fundamental concept that it is used by all types of organizations for all types of bookkeeping, including government institutions and nonprofit organizations.

The double entry system is a powerful tool that can help businesses track their financial performance, identify potential problems, and make informed decisions about their future. It is one of the first accounting principles to be developed and it's now a system that has been used for centuries to provide accurate and reliable financial information.

Even though it is constantly evolving as new technologies enter the game, the basics of the principle remain the same and still shape the new systems and programs used in accounting. The double entry principle is the principle of control, making sure that you keep your accounting statements balanced between the credit and debit transactions which also helps to keep the cash flow accurate.

Matching Principle

One of the most important elements of accounting data is time frames. Most of the accounting data is used later to prepare management reports which are usually trends showing how the business has been performing over time and what can be expected for the future. This is why the matching principle is such an important part of the accounting process. Imagine as a manager, you received a report with a trend of profits over the past year, but you were told that some of the sales figures for April represented actual sales in January, while some of the expenses included in August were incurred in May. Would you still trust this trend to be a good representation of what is happening in the business? Certainly not.

However, the matching principle is there to make sure that this does not happen and every transaction is recorded during the time period it occurs. This means all revenue is recorded at the time of sale and all expenses are recorded when incurred. Let me give you an example from one of my accounting statements from a few years ago. When I was still working in HR, I had to move away from the city I was staying in for four months. During that time, I would pay my rent through checks to the owner of the property.

However, the elderly gentleman never got around to cashing the checks so when I moved back I went and paid for all the past four months in cash and got the checks I had sent back. The mistake I made, however, was recording the total payment for rentals in the month I made the payment and not in the month I incurred the cost. This led to an account breakdown that showed no expense for rent for four months and a huge amount for that one month. This was not accurate, and had I followed the matching principle, I would have put all the expenses for rentals to the periods in which they were incurred.

The matching principle helps to give a much clearer and more concise presentation of the allocation of expenses and revenue. If, in the future I decide to use the data to see the trend in my costs of living, I will be misled since some of the data was not mapped to the period it should have been.

"The matching principle is an accounting concept that dictates that companies report expenses at the same time as the revenues they are related to. Revenues and expenses are matched on the income statement for some time," (CFI Team, 2023, para. 1). This helps to ensure that a company's financial statements are accurate and reflect its true financial performance.

So if a company sells products on credit, it would record the revenue from the sale in the period when the sale is made, even though the cash may not be received until a later period. This is because the company has earned the revenue in the period of the sale, even though it has not yet received the cash.

Similarly, if a company incurs costs for advertising, it would record the expense in the period when the advertising is run, even though the benefits of the advertising may not be realized until a later period. This is because the company has incurred the cost in the period of the advertising, even though it has not yet realized the benefits.

This is a principle you can also use in your small business and your personal life. Be in the habit of recording expenses and revenue as soon as you come across them so that all of your transactions are in the same period all the time. There is another accounting principle that runs parallel to the matching principle and helps to support it in accounting called the "accruals concept." The main difference is that the accruals concept focuses on the accruals and debts of the company while the matching principle looks at more concepts overall.

Accruals Concept

The accruals concept is concerned with the idea that the trend of the financial statements should be accurate over time. It focuses on the idea that all revenue should be recognized when it is realized regardless of when the actual payment is made and all expenses should also be recorded when they are realized and not when the amount is paid. This also looks at prepayments and recognizes that prepayments should be attributed to the period when the company receives the goods or gives the goods to the buyer.

Let's take the example of the T-shirt company, where there was an order for 300 T-shirts to be delivered in a week but the payment could only be made after a month. If you make the T-shirts and give them to the client within the week but then get the money at the end of the month, under the accruals concept, the revenue from that sale should be recognized during the week when the goods were delivered. Even though the cash had not been received yet, the company had already earned the revenue.

In the same way, if you had to purchase T-shirts on credit since you had not yet been paid, promising to only pay when you get the money at the end of the month then you would follow the same principle. Because you have already incurred the cost even though you have not yet paid for it, you should record it then. Even though you have not paid the money yet, you have already incurred the cost and need to account for it.

Consistency Principle

I want you to imagine a situation, where you have the accounts of a business from two years ago and the ones from this past year. Your task is to compare the accounts, but there is a catch. Some areas were treated and recorded differently between the two years. For instance, the accounts are from a country whose currency is not very stable and the fluctuations in inflation are very huge between weeks and even days. Because of this, the first year's accounts were recorded in USD, using the exchange rate at the end of each day to convert all amounts.

In the second year, however, the company did not do this but only changed all the amounts using one rate at the end of the year. In addition to this, the accounts treated assets using the straight line depreciation method during year one but then switched to the declining balance the following year.

The straight line depreciation method is a simple method of calculating depreciation. It assumes that the asset will depreciate at a constant rate over its useful life. The reducing balance depreciation method is a more complex method that assumes that the asset will depreciate at a decreasing rate over its useful life. This leads to the straight line depreciating the exact same amount for the asset every year, while the amount varies under the reducing balance method.

The entire accounting team changed between the two years and the procedures and methods of collecting, storing, and processing data were inconsistent.

Do you think you would be able to make a good comparison between the two sets of accounting statements? I doubt it, and this is why the consistency principle is important. Its job is to help make sure that accounts are prepared and presented the same way from period to period so that it is easy to analyze the accounts, make comparisons, and notice important trends. In the case of the example we gave, the amounts would be different because of the exchange used to convert the amounts and when it was used. Every small element of accounting is important, and by changing these little things, you can end up with two completely different accounts.

While there are so many guiding principles, laws, statute instructions, and regulations on how accounts should be maintained, there will still be differences between how different companies treat their accounts. There is more than one way to be compliant and that means you can get two different results from the same data and have it all be correct. Let's look at an example of this, following our T-shirt business.

Let's say you also make T-shirts for yourself but you almost exclusively sell the T-shirts after you have printed them. Since you are planning to sell the T-shirts after printing them, you can put them down as work in progress instead of finished inventory. However, depending on the management, and how they want it to be recorded, you can also record these T-shirts as inventory since they are finished goods.

These differences can take away so much from the reports and make it nearly impossible to create coherent trends that can be used to make decisions for the company. This is why you should use the same methods for processing and presenting your accounts across time unless there is an issue of compliance. The consistency principle is fundamental.

You can think of all these principles as guiding laws for the world of accounting. Just as there are laws in our physical world that govern everything that happens and how it happens, like the law of gravity, there are also laws in accounting that govern what can happen and how it can happen. The ones we have just gone over are the basic laws of accounting, but there are so many others that govern other areas of accounting and some will work differently depending on the type of business and the local law for the business's geological area of operations.

In the next chapter, we will move on to see how all of this information relates to one of the most important types of accounting. Accounting is as important as it is usable and impactful, and there is no better use for accounting reports than in management. Managers use accounts to see where the business is and to determine where it should go. You are also the manager of your own life and this will help you to see how you can scale down the management accounting information and apply it in your own life.

Chapter 5:

Management Accounting Guiding

Business Decisions

Accounting is a great tool for the management team and for decision-making. Think of a decision you or a business can make that will not have financial implications. Where you are going, what you will eat, what materials to use, who to work with, and when something happens; there will always be finances involved in the process.

I remember the Lecturer who taught me management accounting telling me that every decision is a financial decision. Even the decisions you think have nothing to do with money, are also monetary decisions and will impact your financial health now and into your future. Knowing this, you need to make sure you have considered the impact of what you do and whether it is worth the cost.

This does not mean that you need to avoid everything that brings a cost to your life. Money is meant to serve you and, it's a way for you to improve your life and the experiences that you go through. All you need to do is be aware of the cost of what you are doing and accept that it is the appropriate cost for the experience you are getting.

In this chapter, we will look at how accounting is used for managerial purposes, especially in making decisions for the business and for your personal life. Management accounting is often done to help with three fundamental business problems; cost, budgeting and forecasting, and performance management. Take out your journal again and divide a clean page into three sections. Make note of the three fundamental areas that you should closely monitor for a healthier financial life.

If you have a small business or if you work for a corporation as a manager, then this section is for you. It will help you to use accounting to make the decisions that matter. However, if you do not own a business or work for one, then I want you to consider yourself an enterprise. To be fair, you are. You are like a business in your own right. You use your time and energy to make money and buy resources that you then use to create more energy and even more resources. No one should be left out of this section. This knowledge will be applicable for all areas of life as long you use it right.

Cost Analysis for Decision Making

One of the foremost problems for a business is often its costs. Costs are the expenses that go into running a business and that can be deducted against the income to determine whether the business made a profit or not. Let's say you have a company that makes cereal and you are analyzing the cost of your company. The first thing you should be able to do is separate costs from your investments. In most cases, this is not as easy as it may seem to be since you can make purchases in both cases.

Let's say you use a roller dryer to make your cereal and you buy a new roller dryer. Do you think that would be a cost to you? Tricky one, it will cost you something to buy the roller dryer, but it's not a cost to the business, it's an investment. The main difference, which is not always the case, is that costs are spent money and you lose the value of that as soon as you spend it while investments are still within the company just as another form of value. So if you buy a new car for the company, and a new roller dryer, you do not reduce the value of the company since the assets still have value and since they will even help you to make more money.

Cost analysis is good for so much more than showing the line between your costs and your assets. Most people look at the analysis as input for making decisions and after that, they wait for the plans to be implemented and never go back to the cost analysis again. This is not how you should be using these accounts. Rather, you should use them to track and monitor the decisions you have made to make sure that they are bringing the change you desire. This is not easy as it can identify the flaws in your ideas, but you should see where your mistakes are before they affect the business.

This means you can use cost analysis to manage your plans and decisions and see how well they are doing in real-time. You do not need to wait until the end of the year to cancel some projects and initiatives, all you need to do is keep an eye on the KPIs and see if the costs are responding as you hoped they would when you implemented your measures.

In addition, cost analysis is a good way to evaluate the capacity you have with your resources and find ways to improve the amount you are using. I want you to change how you think of cost analysis from a measure of the business expenses and think of it more as the indicator that there are opportunities to do better.

I learned this concept from someone who used to always say, that if nothing is wrong with the way you are running your business, then that means you cannot get better no matter what. But maybe something is wrong with the way you are doing some things, and maybe if you accept that you can start to look for solutions instead of hiding away. So as either a small business owner, manager, or the average person with a desire to understand how their money works, I want you to look at your accounting reports, especially the cost analysis. I want you to ask yourself what you can do to fix the problem that is there. Consider that you, or your company, has a problem somehow, and the numbers under the costs can be brought down if you try hard enough. Do this for a while and it will completely change the way you look at cost analysis next time.

Budgeting and Forecasting

The main task for managers is to pave the way for the company to succeed. This is done by planning for the future of the company and making sure all the efforts of the company are aimed in the same direction. The managers come up with a vision for the company and from there, they look at the input to see if their goals are realistic, but mostly, to see how they are going to achieve the goals.

The first thing they want to do with the accounting information is look at what the accounts are saying and make a forecast of what is going to happen in the future of your business, your industry, and eventually the entire economy. If you can understand how the industry you operate in is changing, then you will be able to see the opportunities in your future and take full advantage of them.

Forecasting is the process of predicting what the future of the business is going to be like. The foremost use is coming up with a budget for the business. The more you know and can predict the future, the more accurate your budget will be and the less financial stress you will have. Businesses are always trying to come up with a budget that is as close to the actual future costs as possible and that predicts the future income as closely as possible. To help you understand this process better, let's look at what budgeting for companies looks like and how you can do it for your small business or company.

Budgeting

As the person in charge of making the budget, you are responsible for stewarding and directing the finances of the business. This is a great responsibility because failing to direct the resources to the right place will affect the operations of the company and its goodwill, and it might even get you into trouble with the regulation bodies within the government. Budgeting is not just making a list of all the expenses you will have and planning when and how to pay them even though that is its basis. No, budgeting is about managing the costs of the business and keeping track of the flow of the money.

If you know where the money is going to go before it goes there, then you can plan and control how much of it goes there without compromising the quality of services and goods you were getting for the money. This type of budget is called a continuous budget. It is never meant to be concluded or closed. Its main task is to help the management team keep an eye on the coming costs and use that information to figure out ways to reduce the costs or make more money.

On the other hand, we also have zero budgets, which are what the managers will finally come up with after they have removed all the unnecessary costs. A zero budget is zero at the beginning of every year and the manager who wants to use the resources will have to make a justification for everything in the budget. For instance, in Human Resources, the manager might want to increase the labor by 5% because the departments have been making requests for new employees to handle the increased workload.

The Human Resources manager would have to use the request shared by the different departments that want more employees and the salary justification calculation to get the labor budget extended for the following year. This process is effective, especially if done in a collaborative way where all the managers discuss the different requests and try to figure out how much they need to budget for and what they can get by without.

Following the zero budget, management also has to work with capital budgets. Capital budgets are extensive, intended for buying big items such as vehicles, equipment, and buildings. Because the expenditure is very high and affects the capital and valuation of the company, these decisions take time to be made and fully approved. The accounting reports will have to support that the company needs the assets and that there will be a net positive contribution from the asset before management can then agree on the purchase.

Budgets for companies are diverse and offer guidance and visibility. They can help management to better understand the costs of the company and to also control their spending. The best contribution is how they will also help the business to stay vigilant and keep looking forward to what could happen. Accounting is not just a study of what is happening and what has happened in the business, but what is going to happen and how it will affect the business, nation, economy, and investors. This is why technologies that try to predict the markets are on the rise and management is trying its best to gather as much insight as possible into the future of this business.

Performance Reporting

I want to give you two scenarios and want you to consider which you would find more useful as a manager. In scenario one, you have an employee who is doing well, you want to give them a promotion, and you need to decide whether you should pick them over another employee who has been with the organization for longer. This employee has been doing very well, but so has the other one. Both of them have been performing well. The main difference is the one who has been there longer has more knowledge than the new employee.

Scenario two is you have two employees working on a production line. The first line has been with the company for ten years now and they have an output of 3,000 tons every year while the other employee has only been with the company for a year and they have an output of 2,800 tons in their first year. However, it took the employee who has been with the organization longer than five years to output more than 2,500 tons a year and the new employee has been able to do it in the first year.

If you had to pick one employee using either the data in scenario one or scenario two, which are you more comfortable using? Without question, it would be scenario two. While the decision would be just as hard, at least you would have a justification for your decision instead of going off of being subjective.

This is another of the uses of managerial accounts. They help managers associate numbers with the performance of the employees and the business. Performance reporting is the process of gathering, analyzing, and reporting information on the performance of an organization, program, project, or individual. It is used to track progress, identify areas for improvement, and make informed decisions about future actions.

Performance Reports

The accounting team is responsible for preparing and presenting several performance reports as well which will give management more information to work with for different areas of the business. While the reports that apply to a business will differ depending on the type of business and the goals of the business, you will see two or three of the following in any business. You can also note the one that will apply to your business and try to prepare and use it for decision-making.

Financial Reports

Financial reports, as introduced earlier in this book, are the most popular performance reports. Financial reports are also the most useful out of all the reports as they are not only used by the business and its management, but they are used by the government, investors, and even the competitors of the business (in cases where they have visibility). For the most part, the financial reports track the revenue, expenses, assets, liabilities, and profits of the business, giving a good overview of how the business is going.

Operational Reports

For management, the operational reports might just be the most important, tracking all the KPIs that management is concerned about. These are the performance indexes that track how well management is doing their job as well as looking at the everyday operational success like production and efficiencies. In addition to these, you will have elements like customer satisfaction and employee turnover being tracked by these reports, and because of this, every manager should have their eye on these reports throughout the month.

Strategic Reports

Moving up the hierarchy of the organization, we get to strategic management which targets the highest levels of management as they are the ones who set the plan and strategy for the organization. Here, we look at things like the market share of the organization and the long-term goals that the organization would have been pursuing for the period in question.

Compliance Reports

From the sector of accounting that is responsible for auditing, we then get compliance reports. Some regulations govern and track every aspect of the business, from hiring rations and procedures to Carbon Dioxide (CO_2) emissions to the tax and statutory payments required of the organization. It is the job of the accountants to help produce the reports that can keep all of these areas on track for the managers. Failing to keep these reports accurate can have serious negative external impacts for the company, so the internal audit teams will often keep checking these aspects to ensure that the company remains compliant. Compliance is so important, that companies like Bank of America have lost over 30 Billion in fines for failing to be compliant (Husain, 2023).

Risk Reports

One of the most important functions of accounting reports is to identify gaps and possible risks for the future of the company. While risk reports are not usually prepared separately, they can be derived from the results of all the other reports that are available to the management team. As they look through all the other reports, the question they are often trying to answer is if there are any possible threats to the success of the business that have been detected in the reports. Risk reports identify these issues, without relying on the management team to decipher multiple figures.

Management accounting is the most important branch of accounting there is, as it is the application of everything that the accountants would have worked to prepare. Accounts by themselves are not as useful if they are never presented and used for the improvement of the company. If we continue to look at accounting as a story, think of how a story would not be as impactful if it does not carry any lessons learned or meaning that you can relate to your life. That is what accounts would be without the application component and the accountant's interpretation; a bunch of numbers and statements that have little meaning to the organization.

That bridge between the very complex accounting systems and the final report that the managers can understand and use to make decisions for the company is very important and should be preserved. Let's move on to the next chapter and see how the financial statements are prepared.

Chapter 6:

Financial Statements

I know we have discussed how accounting is all about storytelling from the start, but that idea shines brightest in this chapter. Financial statements are like the templates for stories that accountants use to reflect the business's performance. Each of these outlines will help the business and its management to understand key financial elements and make plans to improve the health of the business.

There are a few different financial statements, but we will only look at the most important ones and discuss how they are used. Most importantly, how you can use them yourself. Please grab your journal again and take notes as you read this chapter. I want to challenge you to create these statements for yourself. even a very rough presentation of the statements will do. As you will realize, it's not the actual statements themselves that help you to become better but understanding how and why they are prepared.

Usually, the statements show some relationship between two or more elements and help you to understand the results of comparing the two. For example, you can look at your income versus your expenses and the result will show you whether you have a profit or a loss. Now, let's go and explore this and other concepts that can help you to start preparing your financial statements today.

The Balance Sheet

The most important of all the financial statements by far is the balance sheet. This is a simple document that compares the assets, liabilities, and equity of the business. Because of its function, the balance sheet is the most important statement for most investors and it shows how healthy a business is without going too deep into the rest of the accounts.

A balance sheet is like a screenshot of the financial position of the company at the time that it is prepared. It shows the value of the company and how the assets of the company stand in comparison to the liabilities. According to the article, *What Is a Balance Sheet* (2023), a balance sheet summarizes a company's assets, liabilities, and shareholders' equity at a specific point in time (as indicated at the top of the statement). It is one of the fundamental documents that make up a company's financial statements.

The three main components of a company are its assets, liabilities, and equity, and the balance sheet shows how these interact to give the final value of the business. Assets are things that the company owns, such as cash, inventory, and equipment. Liabilities are things that the company owes, such as accounts payable and loans. Equity is the difference between assets and liabilities. The amount of money that the owners of the company have invested in the business is presented in the balance sheet, making it the most helpful financial document for investors.

A balance sheet must always balance, which means that the total assets must equal the total liabilities plus equity all the time. This makes sense as all the assets—things owned by the company—are financed through liabilities and equity. It would therefore be impossible for there to be more of either. Simply put, the assets of a company are what the company owns, and the liabilities are what the company owes to others, its stakeholders.

Example of a Balance Sheet

1	Balance Sheet as of December 31, 2023	
2	**Assets**	
3	**Current assets:**	
4	Cash and cash equivalents	$10,000
5	Accounts receivable	20,000
6	Inventory	30,000
7	Total current assets	60,000
8	**Long-term assets:**	
9	Property, plant, and equipment	100,000
10	Less accumulated depreciation	(20,000)
11		80,000
12	*Total assets*	*$140,000*
13	**Liabilities**	
14	**Current liabilities:**	
15	Accounts payable	20,000
16	Accrued expenses	10,000
17	Total current liabilities	30,000

18	**Long-term liabilities:**	
19	Notes payable	50,000
20	Total liabilities	80,000
21	**Owner's equity**	
22	Shareholder's equity	60,000
23	***Total liabilities and owner's equity***	***$140,000***

Assets

"A company's assets are things that make it money or give it access to things that no one else has. A right or other access to something is legal. This means that a corporation can use economic resources however it wants, and an owner can stop or limit how those resources are used."(*What Is Asset? Definition of Asset, Asset Meaning*, 2023, para. 3).

As we once covered, the assets are classified into current assets, long-term assets, and intangible assets. On the example balance sheet, you can see these outlined. The current assets are those that can be used and completely spent up in one year, this removes most physical assets like vehicles, land, and buildings as these are often within the business for a long time.

Long-term assets, on the other hand, are those that will not be converted or used within the year but are expected to be used in their current form for a while. In this example, we do not have any, but it is important to remember that we also have intangible assets which do not have physical substance, but which still add value to the company.

The total from this section makes up the total value of the company. In this case, that value as shown in line 12 is $140,000. If the company was to be sold at the time the balance sheet was created, the total value would be around that figure, give or take depending on some elements that would not be captured on the balance sheet.

Liabilities

The second and last part of the example shows the other side of the business, or what if financing the total value of the company. Liabilities are the debts along with other obligations that the business owes other people, excluding the owners. Just like with assets, we have current liabilities, which are debts and loans that the company expects to pay up within one year. These include short-term loans and some of the debts owed to the suppliers.

Following these, we have long-term liabilities, which are debts that are expected to last more than one year. Imagine a situation where you get a loan of $100,000 to buy more equipment for the business. The additional equipment would be an asset, and the value of the company would go to $240,000 from $140,000. However, since the asset was sponsored by a loan, there would be a new liability of $100,000 in the form of the loan and this would keep the balance sheet balanced.

Liabilities cannot be overlooked because they are payments that the company has to make by obligation. If a company decides to close, the assets would all be dissolved and used to pay off all the liabilities first and then the remaining amount is what will be given to the owners of the company. The amount of liabilities and the owner's equity show how healthy the company is, in other words, they show how much of the company is owned by the company's owners.

Owner's Equity

This is the figure that matters the most as it represents the amount the owners of the company would get if the company were to close. This is actually what makes the balance sheet very important. Most people consider the ratio between the liabilities and equity to be the most important measure of how good a business is for investment. This figure shows control, and if more than half of your assets are backed by liabilities, this effectively means that more than half of your company is not yours but belongs to people you owe.

By looking at the balance sheet, the investor can also get a good idea of what the return on investment is for the project and use that to decide if they want to be a part of the company or not. It is very hard to lure investors to your company, so you want to make sure your accounts are as attractive as possible to new investors. Besides the investors, balance sheets are used by creditors, and other interested parties to assess the financial health of a company and decide if they want to work with that company. They can be used to compare the financial performance of a company over time or to compare the financial performance of different companies and determine which would be a better option to work with.

Here are some things that might be good to know about preparing the balance sheet. The first is that assets are usually listed in order of liquidity, which is a measure of how quickly they can be converted into cash for use. The assets that can easily be converted to cash are listed first and the ones that would be harder to convert go last.

Next, the liabilities are listed in order of the date by which they need to be paid. So the liabilities that will be paid sooner will go first, while those who are still to be paid later, will go last. This makes it easier for investors and other interested parties to see how much the short-term loans of a company are and how small the long-term obligations are as well.

Following all of these, equity goes to the bottom of the balance sheet, and its amount changes to balance out the equation. It goes up when the liabilities go down and then it goes down when the company gets more liabilities than the addition of assets. Typically, the balance sheet would be prepared on a page with two sides with either side having one of the sides of the question and the total at the bottom always having to be the same.

I suggest you take the time to look at some balance sheets online and go through them to try to see what you can pick out. As you go through them, remember that balance sheets are a good tool for understanding the financial health of the company. Ask yourself if you think a company is healthy based on its accounts and try to compare two or more companies at a time.

Profit and Loss Statement

The main purpose for most businesses is to make a profit. Even those that do not directly set out to make a profit, set out to make sure they do not lose money but have enough to fulfill the objectives of the company. This is why the company need to understand how much of a profit or loss was recognized and how. The profit and loss statement is exactly designed for this as a report that shows how the company lost money through expenses and how the company made money through sales and other income sources.

The equation for this report is Net Profit and Loss = ((Total Revenue + Additional Income) – (Cost of Products and Services + Operating Costs)) – (Interests + Taxes + Depreciation + Amortization)(Cohen, 2021). I know this one has a few elements, but we can go through this one by one and see what they mean so that you can duplicate the exercise for yourself or your small business. Let's look at all the elements of the equation first.

Net profit or loss are the two possible outcomes of any venture. On rare occasions, the business can break even, which means the equation has come out with a net total of zero, but this is very unique. A profit is when there is money made from the operations of the business while a loss shows that the business has lost more money than it has made. But I have a question for you before we go further. Let's say you have a small business that is worth $1,000 and makes you about $200 every week. If one of the weeks you decide to buy a machine that will expand your business' capacity for $500 and still make $200 in that week then can you say you had a loss of $300? I want you to think about this and write out your response in your journal.

Total Revenue and Additional Income

Moving on, let's look at the sources of revenue and income. A company gets money often through selling services as goods and this is what we refer to as revenue. However, there are other ways a business can make money other than the revenue that they receive for selling their services and products. This is considered additional income and it is added to the revenue at the end of each month.

Additional income can include things like interest given to the company from the bank or their suppliers. You can have instances where the company charges their suppliers for failing to comply with their agreements or where employees are penalized and have to pay a fee. All of these kinds of payments would not be part of the regular revenue. Anything that is not the company's core service or product does not count as revenue but rather as additional income.

Think of this from your life's perspective. Let's say you meet with an old friend and after catching up for a bit, they slip a $100 bill into your pocket and say get yourself a drink tomorrow. This money is not a direct reflection of your efforts throughout the week. You cannot tag it as part of your salary even though you still need to account for it. You can account for it as additional income so that you do not overstate the outcome of your efforts, and so that you also do not understate how much money you have received.

Cost of Products and Services and Operating Costs

The creation of any product or service is going to have direct expenses and these make up the main costs of the business. If you have a paper-making company, then the cost of buying, transporting, and grinding timber is your main expense and you will have it consistently as long as you continue with production. If you run a call center on the other hand, you will need to pay for all the software and systems that you need plus the internet and labor that is taking the calls. These costs are very important because they can also be used to measure your business's efficiency with resource management.

The best way to explain efficiency is with a company that does production and uses raw materials for their products. Consider the company that makes T-shirts and they have about one ton of fabric that has to be thrown away after making 100,000 T-shirts. If the company can leave less waste fabric after achieving the same number of T-shirts, then they are more efficient with their resources.

However, it is important to always have a holistic view of the process, especially since you can reduce one cost by raising another in some cases. Imagine if, with our example, there would need to be more advertising at about the same cost as what the company fabric waste cost. This would mean the waste reduction is not translating to savings just a transfer of the cost to another area of the business.

Operating costs are the costs of everything that needs to happen to make the product or service available. You can see this as the cost of all the actions that support the production of the product. Things like cleaning machinery, the electricity, water, rentals, and everything else that has to be paid to keep the business going.

Interests, Taxes, Depreciation, and Amortization

The second group of expenses are not directly related to the production or operations process, but they are costs that should be attributed to that period nonetheless, and they affect the profit or the loss of the company. Imagine if I told you I made $400 last month on my little business but then left out that I had to pay interest for the loan I took at $200 and that I had to pay taxes of $20. The result would not be a good representation of how my business is doing. This is one of the things accountants are trying to avoid. The financial books must be the most accurate possible representation of the position of the company.

The most popular of all these costs is interest, which can be paid for many different things. Imagine you receive some raw materials on loan and have to pay it back over four months with an interest of 10% every month. That 10% will be a cost recorded in each of those periods since it's money you are losing. Interest, however, is not only paid on materials taken on loan, sometimes you can take loans from financers to help your business and the interest on these loans would be recorded here as well.

In addition, we have taxes, the inevitable cost for every business and individual. Taxes are paid to the government in line with the rules that govern the tax law for your state or country. Tax is imposed to make companies pay for negative externalities that they cannot factor into their accounting system otherwise. The tax will be calculated based on how much the company has made, and the field of operations it is in. This means that if a company's negative externalities are greater, they pay more in taxes. So even if they are the same size and make the same amount of money, a company that is mining will be taxed higher than a call center.

Furthermore, there is a general loss of value over time as the assets get used through the operations. This natural wear and tear of company assets is referred to as depreciation (see line 10 on the Balance Sheet example above). Let's say a company bought a car four years ago that is being used to go and buy raw materials every two days. The car will slowly lose its value until it has a net value of zero and this process needs to be recorded. Remember, the value of assets is one of the components of the balance sheet, therefore, if you do not have the actual value of the assets at the end of the month, then you will have a hard time creating an accurate balance sheet.

In a nutshell, the profit and loss accounting will show you how much money your business is making or losing by comparing its revenues to its expenses for the period in question. It goes without saying how important it is for the business to know how much it is making or losing through its operations, as this is the most important thing for most businesses.

By comparing the statements for one period over another, you can see the improvements or lack thereof between the periods being compared. If you have a couple of statements from different times, you can also create trends that can help you understand what has been happening in the business over time. This is, as you will recall, a very important element of managerial accounts.

Since the profit and loss statement is prepared for sharing with external stakeholders as well, it can be used when applying for loans or financing as it shows lenders how much cash the company has available and how it is being used. The investors of the company would be especially interested in knowing if the company is making profits with their money or if they are not. Another group that will also have interests in this account are regulatory bodies from the government who audit the accounts and also use them to verify the tax being paid by the company.

Cash Flow Statement

Cash is the single most important element in a company. If a company were the human body, cash would be in some way, like the blood. It flows throughout the company to keep it alive. Every function and operation costs the business money, and can be represented as cash. Some of these operations will use the cash while others will support the ones that bring in cash to make sure the business remains alive.

I cannot express how important it is for you to understand how the cash is flowing in your business. You need to know how much of it you received and where it applies. This statement single-handedly is the main reason most small businesses fail. They do not track their cash flow carefully, so they could even think they are making a profit when in fact they are not.

There are three parts to any cash flow statement; operating activities, investing activities, and financing activities. With the help of an example, we are going to look at all three of these and also see how you can create your cashflow statement. Below is an example of a cash flow statement for reference as we go through and explain the different sections of a cash flow statement.

Just a few things to note as you go through the statement. All amounts in parenthesis are being deducted while all the other amounts are being added. So, for example, in line 4, the 10,000 is being deducted while the 20,000 from line 3 is being added.

Example of a Cash Flow Statement

Line	Cash Flow Statement For KLS Company For the Year Ending December 31, 2023	
1	Net income	$100,000
2	Adjustments to reconcile net income to net cash provided by operating activities:	
3	Depreciation and amortization	$20,000
4	Increase in accounts receivable	(10,000)
5	Increase in inventory	(15,000)
6	Decrease in accounts payable	10,000
7	Net cash provided by operating activities	$105,000
8	Investing activities:	
9	Purchase of equipment	(50,000)
10	Sale of land	20,000

11	Net cash used by investing activities	(30,000)

12	**Financing activities:**	
	Issue of common stock	50,000
13	Payment of dividends	(20,000)
14	Net cash provided by financing activities	30,000
15	Net increase in cash and cash equivalents	$85,000
16	Cash and cash equivalents at the beginning of the year	10,000
17	Cash and cash equivalents at the end of the year	$95,000**g**

Operating Activities

The operations section looks at the cash that the organization makes from its core activities. If you are running a production company, this will look at all the sales and revenue you make from your everyday activities. The biggest and most consistent source of income for almost all companies is the profit from operations, which is shown as the net income after calculations. This is the main figure for the operating activities. The other entries, as shown in the example, are either additions or subtractions to the cash received from the revenue.

The interesting entry for this section is on line five, which shows an increase in inventory. Inventory is a good thing, it's a product that the company can sell and make money, but unfortunately, it is not cash until it has been sold. It costs money to make more inventory, so an increase in inventory will be a decrease in cash.

Investing Activities

Investing activities often involve huge amounts of money and are completed after careful consideration from the company's management. Because of this, these entries are very rare and only show up now and then. Here, we are looking at all money made from selling assets of the company and spent buying assets for the company.

I will note at this point that this statement is not trying to show the profitability of the company, but the cash at hand only. In some instances, the company can use a lot of money buying assets, such that they have very little cash at the end of the period. This is not necessarily the same as having failed to make a profit, a process we look at in the profit and loss accounts.

Financing Activities

The last section looks at the activities that finance the operations of the business. Sometimes the business will realize that they need to get more capital to sustain or even expand their business and this is where it is recorded. This section records all the efforts of the business to finance itself and increase its cash and capital without selling inventory or engaging in its core activities. It also records how the business loses cash sometimes to payments from financing activity. Some activities come with obligations like dividends while loans come with interest and all of these reduce the cash flow of the company.

Benefits of the Cashflow Statement

There are many benefits to the cash flow statement, but the main one is how it helps the business to see where all the cash it received came from and how it was used. Think back to when we talked about the matching principle in accounting. We learned that we are not supposed to prepare the accounts based on when a payment is made, but rather when the service or product is sold or received. While we now know the benefits and reasons for the matching principle, you also need to have visibility to see how much money you receive and where the money goes throughout the period in question.

This statement seeks to answer those questions and more by showing a clear presentation of every transaction that brought in or took money in that period. Another benefit of the cash flow account is that it helps the manager to see how much cash they have at the specific time of preparation.

Cash is measurable and just because you or your company is wealthy, does not mean you have the cash to make the purchases you want. The business will have budgets and obligations, so the accountant needs to make sure they keep an eye on the amount of cash available at all times. This makes the statement the perfect measure for the company's liquidity and financial health by depicting the company's ability to meet its short-term obligations and maintain its overall financial health.

The Wild Card

Now, I know what you might have thought when you went through the example. How come line 3-Depreciation and amortization is negative even though depreciation is a cost to the company and line 4-Increase in accounts receivable is negative even though its income to the company. Let's look at these two wild cards separately and see what we can learn.

To start with, depreciation is not even a cash transaction, so it does not affect the cash flow at all. Depreciation is perceived loss of value, but cash does not actually reduce from the company because of depreciation. I know this makes it even more complicated, but there is a good reason we still add it in the cash flow statement. When we added the amount in line 1-Net income, we used an amount which was calculated through the profit and loss statement.

When this amount is calculated, depreciation is considered as part of the operating expenses that reduce the value of the equipment and assets used for producing the services and products. It's a cost that is deducted from the amount even though it has no effect on the cash that the business has. And therein lies our answer, we are now adding back the amount that we deducted from the net income because—for cash flow purposes—it should not have been deducted in the first place.

The same logic applies to why we have a negative amount for the accounts receivable. Accounts receivable show the sales that we made but which have not been paid yet, so an increase in accounts receivable is add to the profit made for the period. However, this is money added to the net income even though it does not increase the cash flow of the company in that moment, so to keep the cash flow statement accurate, we have to remove it from the net income.

These are the main statements in accounting and you need to know what each shows and how to prepare them. There are so many sides to every business, you need to be able to understand the financial situation of every department so that you get a clear picture.

You need to be able to read and understand the story of the business you are interested in and now, you should be able to. I suggest you go online and look up the financial statements that have been published by some publicly traded companies. Using these principles, I want you to check and see if there are any similarities between the companies, and if you understand the statements better now that you have an overview of the reports.

This is such a fundamental idea in accounting. If you do not understand any of these ideas, then you will have a hard time understanding the financial statements of the company. Since we use this information to make wise decisions for the company, this means you might fail to make the appropriate decisions you need to because you do not understand the accounts. If you do not fully understand some of the ideas we have gone over, as long as you keep reading and learning, I know everything will fall into place.

Heading into the next chapter, you will learn about some of the most important concepts in accounting and how they tie in with all the functions we have explored.

Chapter 7:

Advanced Accounting Concepts

Let's look at more accounting ideas that can help to solidify your understanding of accounting. There are so many layers to accounting, and you can always go a step further depending on what you want to use accounting for. Every scenario will have its own separate set of requirements and therefore a combination of principles that will need to be applied.

Think of it this way, if you are running a small business locally that trades one product in one currency, that would be very different from someone who is trading and manufacturing a couple of products that are being sold all over the world in different currencies. The levels of complexity will go up as you scale your business up and add more sophistication.

The concepts we go over in this chapter are some unique ideas that might not apply to every situation, but that are good to know. We will cover international accounting, financial derivatives, accounting ethics, and lastly accounting information systems. All of these concepts can be applied to any business but they are more useful for large businesses.

I always like to start and end every accounting idea with the individual. You are as good at accounting as you are at using it in your personal life. If you cannot bring these concepts to your everyday tasks and financial management then you will have a very hard time making the ideas work in a big organizational environment. We will also look at simplified examples of these concepts so that you can incorporate them confidently into your everyday life. Remember, accounting is an everyday activity. You are always accounting for something. If you are not, then you are missing valuable information.

That being said, join me as we explore these somewhat deep, but very useful concepts. As always, I invite you to write down everything that crosses your mind and ensure your journal is a supplement to this book that will help you to go back in and reinforce any concept when you need to. Write down what sticks out to you, what raises more questions, and what makes you happy. This is a learning journey after all, one that will leave you with a great understanding of accounting when we are done.

International Accounting

Let's take Ray as an example. After working hard on his product for years, he was finally able to start selling it in Texas where his factory was located. However, he was able to expand his production even further, so he started to supply the product to all the states and had the entire country covered by the end of the decade. Now, Ray is thinking about expanding the business into other countries, starting with South Africa and China, but he would love to have his product in every country eventually.

As he was moving his product into the different states, he noticed that there were some laws and regulations here and there that differed ever so slightly and this would often affect how he would account for his sales and production costs. He priced the items differently depending on the state and also had some labels changed to best match the state in which he was planning on selling the products.

Since realizing all of this, Ray is afraid there might be regulations and laws in the other counties that will divert from what he is used to, impact the consistent presentation of the accounting, and make it hard for him to manage his business effectively. These fears are genuine, and Ray should take some time to learn more about the local accounting regulations before he starts to enter these territories. Beyond that; however, he needs to learn about international accounting and understand the regulations and standards that govern all things accounting all over the world.

After Ray learns about the accounting standards of the country he wants to move into, he will then need to merge that with the accounting standards of the country he is already in, and also consider the international accounting standards. There are so many things at play when you start a business venture in another country such that you cannot afford to wing it. There are considerations around acquisitions, transportation, import tax, and investor benefits among many other concepts that might apply to the business.

In Ray's case, he would need to get an expert in South Africa to walk him through the main concepts that make up the accounting standards and then help him to set up an accounting system that will both honor those regulations and also help Ray to keep a good eye on his business.

Accounting standards primarily deal with the preparation and presentation of financial statements for companies that operate in their countries. This is done so that the government can have a good idea of how the economy is performing and also know how much they should be taxing each company. The government will then audit these companies to make sure they are preparing their accounting statements according to the standard.

Take a situation where the country has a law stating all medical and housing benefits to employees are not taxed, but Ray does not know this. The company can then pay tax on benefits where they otherwise should not have done so leading to unnecessary loss and inaccurate accounting. On the other hand, if Ray misses some regulations he can understate his profits and pay less tax than he is supposed to. If the regulating body finds this out, the company can be fined huge amounts of money in addition to all the amounts they have to pay back. This is why it is important to know the accounting standards of the country or state of operations.

Understanding international standards will help to get a good understanding of the regulations that generally work for most countries. If there is something local to that country only, you might not be off by a lot as long as you are following the international accounting standard. It is not as easy as reading the accounting standards and you will know what you need to record. You need to take time both studying and using the standards to eventually truly understand how to use them.

Because of how the world is moving to online platforms for commerce, you might need to understand how this works in your personal life as well. I had a friend who started doing some work for a company in

Australia while in Nigeria but then moved to Canada after a while. When he got to Canada, the amount he was receiving before as his net through the transfers now needed to be taxed as part of his income as well. There are so many ways the international guideline accounting standards will affect how the companies you work for interact with you depending on your location.

Compliance is a major function of accounting. The accountant is not just doing your accounting for your business so you can make good decisions and you can have an idea of how your business is going. They also have to do accounting for others; such as the government and your shareholders for example. They therefore have a legal obligation to make sure your accounting statements are accurate for these groups of people and if they do not comply with the accounting standards, there can be legal action taken against them and the business which can include heavy fines and penalties.

One of the main benefits of international accounting standards is how they can help investors understand accounting statements recorded in other countries. This creates a standard accounting language so that there is no confusion about what is considered when creating accounting reports and what should be included in them. Now more than ever, it has become possible for people to invest in companies that are all over the world. It's easier to travel to these places, but it's also easier to connect to the communities online and this creates a chance to have transnational investments.

Financial Derivatives

Financial derivatives are contracts that derive their value from an underlying asset, such as a stock, bond, or commodity. You can think of them as insuring the price of a certain asset will not change in the future. Let's look at an example that demonstrates this idea. Imagine you are a manufacturer making cheese and your main ingredient is milk. Let's say you buy most of your milk from a farmer in your city who also happens to sell some of their milk on the open market.

Since the prices of commodities like milk will often change depending on availability and demand, the farmer is always adjusting his price according to the market. Now imagine a situation where the farmer thinks that the price of milk is going to go down while you think the price of milk is going to go up. In this case, you can get into an agreement with the farmer where they agree to sell you the milk at the current price for the next six months, regardless of the fluctuating economy.

Since the farmer thinks the price will go down, then it's okay for them to sell the product at the current price in the future, and since you think the price will go up, you would rather secure the product at the current price. This is a simple version of how financial derivatives work, but there is so much more to it. In the same example, imagine the farmer does not have enough storage facilities to store a lot of milk and needs to sell it before it goes bad within a day of production. In this case, it would be beneficial for them to have a sure customer who will take the product at a price that they already know.

This gives them assurance that they will not fail to find a customer for the milk and it also gives you the certainty that you will be able to find the milk and not have to halt production. Other benefits like being able to budget more effectively with a consistent rate, also leads people to enter these agreements and preserve the value of their products. This opens up another dimension of financial derivatives; they are often used to hedge risk or speculate on the future price of an asset.

Financial derivatives can be used to mitigate risk by allowing investors to lock in a price for an asset in the future which gives some level of control. This can be helpful if the investor is concerned about the potential for the asset's price to decline so they can be sure of the price of the asset regardless of how the economy fluctuates.

In addition to this, financial derivatives can also be used to speculate on the future price of an asset. This is done by buying or selling a derivative contract hoping that the price of the underlying asset will move in the desired direction. Going back to our example with milk; imagine someone is watching the economy and they are very sure that the price of milk is going to go up. If they can find the farmer and convince them to sell them the milk at the current price , then they can profit off the lower price if their prediction proves correct. This is always a gamble though as the markets are not that easy to anticipate. There is so much that could happen and change the projection of the price trends for the asset.

Even for the sharpest accountant, financial derivatives can be complex instruments. It is important to understand the risks involved before trading them and make sure you consult as many other experts as you can. There are so many risks with financial derivatives, and if you do not have to use them, you might want to stay away from them.

The biggest risk you face will be that the price of the asset will go against your prediction. Since the price can only go up or down, that means there is about a fifty-fifty chance that you could be wrong every time you make a decision. In addition, you do not have any control over what will affect the bonds in most cases. Imagine you have agreed to buy milk at the set price for next year but then, one of the biggest companies that make cream using milk shuts down.

Because of the shutdown, there will be more milk available than you could have predicted and the price is going to go down while you still buy the milk at the same high price that you agreed to. Do not bet on the market, unless you have to and unless you have control over the outcome.

The risk Imagine you are the farmer and the company that closed was your biggest customer set to buy all of your milk in the coming days. This can ruin your process and require you to do things you otherwise would not have had to, like getting extra storage. Besides this, financial derivative contracts are vulnerable to fraud, and other operational risks such that facilitating them will often cost a bit of money.

I know we have been looking at this from a corporate perspective, but you do this in your personal life as well. Think about it, have you ever bought something because you thought the price would go up even though you did not need it then? Or. maybe you have passed up buying something because you believed the price would go down. The only difference is you were not able to make agreements with the sellers to give you the item at a future date at a fixed price, but it is essentially the same concept.

In conclusion, you should always consult with a professional before you start trading financial derivatives, and even then, you should be fully aware of the information you approve. Financial derivatives can be used to hedge risk, speculate on future prices, and generate income: Financial derivatives can generate income through capital gains, which are the profits made when selling a financial derivative for more than its original purchase price.

The other use of derivatives is speculating on future prices. Financial derivatives can also be used to speculate on future prices of assets and other equity items. For example, an investor might buy a call option on a stock if they believe that the stock price will increase in the future. If the stock price does increase, the investor will make money on the call option.

There is so much more to this system of accounting, including swapping and futures. I encourage you to continue studying more about these concepts if this is a branch of accounting that interests you. You can make a lot of money as an investor if you master the seemingly simple but challenging art of financial derivatives.

Accounting Information Systems

Earlier we talked about how one of the responsibilities of an accountant is recording data accurately and then presenting it according to the set standards for the business and its stakeholders. Fortunately for the accountant, there are accounting information systems that can help with these processes. We will look at these processes in depth in a later chapter, but for now, let's look at how they aid the accounting system in creating more accurate and helpful books.

According to Fontinelle (2022), an accounting information system (AIS) is a system that a business uses to collect, store, manage, process, retrieve, and report its financial data. This data can then be used by accountants, consultants, business analysts, managers, chief financial officers (CFOs), auditors, regulators, and tax agencies.

The main advantage of accounting information systems is that they improve accuracy and efficiency in recording and processing financial transactions by automating many of the tasks involved in these administrative components. This had been a problem for accountants for ages, as businesses got bigger, the process of using actual journals to record transactions became more tedious. The business also got to a stage where multiple transactions were happening all over and they all needed to be recorded, but having a system in place meant the accountant did not have to record every transaction one by one.

The only thing the accountant had to then do, was make sure the systems were calibrated to record the information correctly and to use the provided information to prepare the books for the company. The introduction of an AIS also gives other people the opportunity to take control of their financial transactions. If they are accurate and easy systems to use, then people will not always need to have an accountant there with them to make large purchases. They can record their purchase and have it authorized in the system and then send the request to accounting for payment. The system can also allow them to go back and add receipts and invoices to close the request for the purchases.

There are financial benefits through cost saving when you have a system that saves time on inputting data, reconciling accounts, and generating reports. In addition to saving time, this will also help to keep the accounts accurate. A system can easily pick when the receipt is not tallying with the amount requested and flag it; it can also flag anything suspicious for the accountant to investigate, meaning there is less likelihood of error.

At this point, almost all major companies have moved to a digital information system for their accounting instead of the manual process. However, if you are starting with accounting, I would advise you to do it in a physical journal manually recording all transactions and working out the solutions. By doing this, you are training yourself to understand how the final reports come to be and how to record and understand what the system will be doing. You might have a hard time noticing if there is an error in your system if you have never taken the time to do accounts by hand.

I hope you have been recording the ideas that stand out to you in your journal as we have been going along . I want to remind you that this is your financial journey. This process can drastically change how you view, understand, and manage your finances, you should get as much out of it as you can. Accounting is not closed off to the few who went to university anymore. It's for everyone, including you, and it will seriously change your life.

Moving on with the idea of AIS, another point to note is how they improve the security of your data and keep it safe for reviews. These systems can be duplicated on multiple servers, making it easy to have copies of the data stored in the cloud and on a main server. There is also greater access control since the company can control both who has physical access to the servers and who can log into the cloud and access the records.

In addition to this, you can look for the records you want more easily since the search index can filter out what you are not interested in and get you the results that you want. Accounting systems are an accountant's best friend, they will help them to improve accuracy, consistency, and timeliness, identify trends, and make better decisions on how to allocate and manage resources.

Accountants Must Be Independent in Their Work

Since accountants work for companies and are directly reporting to people, it can be very hard for them to remain independent in their work. While an accountant is being paid by the company and doing work for the company, there is a higher diligence to the governing bodies of accounting practice that the accountant must follow as much as they can. This is good even for the company because it protects them from things like fraud.

An accountant should always make sure their only ally are the accounting principles while everything else is first seen through the eyes of compliance and honoring regulations. I believe that being independent is not only for the accountants, but everyone who handles and uses the reports and data provided from accounting should also carry the same integrity and impartiality expected of the accountant. One thing I have learned through years of working in different positions and for different companies is that, the integrity and reliability of the data is inseparable from that of the people handling the data.

Accountants Must Maintain Confidentiality

Being an accountant is not easy. There are so many thin lines and you cannot afford to step on any of them. There is a level of importance that comes with that line of work and. unfortunately, it also demands high and often hard-to-maintain standards for the accountant. The accountant should have integrity as much as knowing and follow the rules that guide the accounting statements themselves.

One of the issues to watch out for as an accountant is how to balance being honest and accurate in the reporting, while also maintaining the confidentiality of the company. An accountant signs a nondisclosure agreement and this will require them to keep the company's information safe and secure. They should not, in a personal or professional capacity, share the company's private information.

This can then be a hard one to keep since part of the job of an accountant is to make and provide accounting statements for the public in some cases. However, the more you learn in the field, the easier it will become for you to tell the difference between sharing confidential information and sharing accurate and acceptable accounting reports.

As an accountant, you should be ethical and honest . You have such a great responsibility as an accountant and need to foster trust. You have the task to create meaning out of the transactions of the business and what you deliver is what the company, management, investors, government, and all other interested parties will see as the truth about the financial health of the business.

Even when you get into positions and situations where you are asked to manipulate the accounting statements to tell a certain narrative that is not true, you need to stick with your ethics and prepare the statements as true as you know how. There is nothing more virtuous than the ability to withstand the temptation to misuse your knowledge and influence as an accountant. Even when you do not get recognition from anyone, you still owe yourself the respect it takes to maintain your integrity.

Now, let's look at the process through which you interact with one of the groups that will be using your unbiased and accurate information, the investors. Almost every big business has its own set of investors, people who put money into the business to make the goals come to life. There is so much you need to know as an investor or accountant who will end up working with investors and we will cover everything in the coming chapter.

Chapter 8:

Investments and Risk Management

One of the most important aspects of accounting is investments, the process where people put their money into a product or business and expect to get profits from it. Real estate is a common example of an investment with growth potential. Investments will help the business to get the cash it needs to get running and expand while also allowing the investors to get more money for their investments. Unfortunately, the business needs to convince the investors that their money will be safe and that it will be able to grow through the business.

Accounting is used by businesses to prove to the investors that the business has been doing well and that it will continue to do so with time. This assures the investors that their money is safe with the company. But this is not where it stops. Accounting will also help you to make decisions for investments in your personal life as well. Understanding the basics of accounting will help you to invest your money in different areas of your life carefully.

Risk Management

The world is riddled with risk, especially when we look at the commercial world. Did you know nearly 50% of all businesses fail within the first five years of operations? (Carter, 2021). This means that if you are starting a business, there is already a fifty percent chance that it will not be successful, and if you do not have the accounting knowledge needed to avert this you will likely fail.

Risk management protects your assets and finances by helping you make informed decisions about how to allocate your resources and manage your risks. You are always choosing how to allocate three main elements, even when you are not a business. Each day, you need to decide how you are going to use your money, time, and your energy. If you do not use any of these effectively you will end up missing out on potential success.

Proper and well-defined risk management systems will help to protect your assets and finances by allowing you to identify potential risks, assess their likelihood and impact, and take steps to control them. Imagine you hear that a storm is coming that could potentially affect your area. This is the equivalent of the information that you can get from your risk management accounting. You will be able to tell if the economic environment predicts an increase or a decrease in the value of your assets and property among other metrics. You will also be able to tell if your business is going to be impacted and whether the outcome is going to be positive or negative.

Let's go back to the weather example. If you hear that there is a storm coming to your area, what will you do? Nothing is certainly not the right answer, but it is also not obvious what your response should be. This shows us that it's not just about you having the knowledge that risk management gives, but you should also know how to react when you receive the information. Some of the things you can start to consider when you are anticipating a storm include moving some of your property around, especially your family, and reinforcing the main structure, your house. You can also be on the lookout and keep checking the news so you know how the risk evolves and keep making your decisions based on the new information.

This is also how you should view and treat your investments. You need to constantly assess the risk and make informed decisions that are based on the most current information. Accounting is in itself a risk assessment too. All of the types of accounting books and ledgers we have discussed are another way of completing risk assessment, and this is especially true when you look at the books over time. For example, if you look at the profit and loss statement for a company for the last 10 years, you should be able to anticipate how the company will likely perform in the coming years.

Through trends, accounting can help us to see which businesses are at risk and which ones have the potential to succeed. Like we said earlier, anything that can be applied to your business, can also be applied to your personal life, including this concept of risk management. Look at the trends around how you spend your money and invest it, and then try to see how you have been doing over time. There are so many insights that you might miss until you start to look at the accounting data critically. Some businesses that are not making a lot of money might think they are when they do not look at the accounts and study them carefully.

Benefits of Risk Management

Risk management might be a small part of the accounting process, but its benefits cannot be downplayed. This is one of the things that will have a direct impact on the future of the investments we make, and therefore can affect the course of your life either positively or negatively. The biggest advantage of risk management is that it helps you to reduce the likelihood of losses by avoiding costly mistakes and ensuring that you are prepared for anything that comes your way. One of the two main reasons for accounting is reducing losses, and this means that risk management is already contributing greatly to your life and business.

Remember that accounting reports are also what investors use to decide if they want to give money to a business or not. Now, I want you to imagine you are an investor and you find out the company you are about to invest in has been hit by different crises year after year, and they have had to consistently rebuild afterward. Even if the business is doing fairly well at that moment, how will you feel knowing that the business could be hit by another crisis and they likely will not see it coming? You can see how this would be concerning for investors.

On the other hand, you can be the company that takes initiative and prepares every time there is an anticipated change in the economic environment. Even if you are caught in some of the problems the economy throws your way, you will still be in a good position for the investors because they know you are always monitoring the environment and will do your best to avert disasters in the first place. This will greatly improve your company's reputation as one with good crisis management.

Investors might be the most important stakeholders in any business, but the regulating bodies for that business have more influence. Failing to keep them satisfied will inevitably lead to the closing of the business. Every business is regulated by the government through several organizations that seek to protect the consumers of the end products and the investors. The statutory regulations and guidelines need to be met to avoid having your business penalized or fined, which will be both costly and affect your reputation.

Risk management will help you to see where there are gaps that can lead to noncompliance with the regulations that govern the business. Like I always say, these ideas will also apply to your personal life and having this basic understanding will help you to avoid some problems in the future. Risk management in your personal life can help you to identify where you need to make adjustments to your taxable income so that you are not subject to litigation for tax evasion in the future. Individual income and expenses, just like those for businesses, are also guided and regulated by the government, so the same level of awareness is needed regardless of whether you are a professional accountant, someone running a small business, or an individual.

Essentially, risk management will help you to comply with regulations by identifying and assessing risks, and then developing and implementing controls to mitigate those risks. This can help you avoid fines, penalties, and other consequences of noncompliance while confirming your integrity in the process. No one wants to work with companies that are not trustworthy.

Business is all about finding a problem and offering a solution that is affordable and sustainable to resolve that problem. Businesses themselves, however, are also riddled with problems that management needs to identify and find solutions for before they affect operations or the bottom line of the business. Risk management is the process through which the business will find areas that need fixing even before the trouble begins. You cannot take this for granted; it's always easier to fix the boat before the storm.

Transparency

Imagine you go to work along with your other five teammates and the boss says they will give a bonus based on your labor. After the project, the employer chooses one person and gives them an amount of money in secret and states that they must distribute it equally among the rest of the team. The catch is that you have no way of knowing how much this one person has been given.

Would you be okay with this system of operation? Would you trust that the amount you are getting is actually what you should be getting even though you have no way of proving it? Well, not having proper and transparent accounting reports is very similar to this situation. In both situations, there is mistrust and there could be some fraud as well.

Even if you were the one in charge and had to share the money among your teammates— knowing if you kept 90% of the money, no one would know—what would you do? You could act with integrity and distribute all the money evenly. Or, you could look for a way to justify your actions and start by taking a bit from everyone until you are holding on to as much as you can without completely losing the team.

Imagine an investor is about to bring millions of dollars into a company expecting a return, but the company will choose to declare any amount as profits that they want. You can see how this would not end well for both the company and the investors. If the company does this, then no one will want to work with them for fear of being cheated out of their money. The accounts must be transparent and verified by auditors to make sure the investors know what they are getting into when they sign up to work with the company.

If investors have confidence in the financial reports being provided, they will also have confidence in the company that is providing these statements. In fact, this could affect the entire economy of a country or industry. If the accounting regulations of a nation or an industry are not strict enough to ensure transparency, then most of the investors will end up staying away or pulling out as the risk becomes greater that the potential benefits.

Transparency will help the stakeholders to have a clear understanding of a company's financial situation. When stakeholders can see that a company is being transparent about its financial information, they are more likely to trust that the company is performing honestly and ethically. How can you bring this into your own life? Not by making your financial transactions transparent to everyone for one, naturally. There is a way you can bring this to your personal life however, and that is by being transparent with yourself. I cannot emphasize this enough. You need to be confident enough to go through your accounting statements and write down what trends you see.

If you are not clear and accurate with your own financial statements, then you will not be able to gain control over your financial life. If you learn to manage your own money responsibly, then you can also learn to manage other people's resources and will become a good accountant in the end. This concept becomes even more important when you start to run a small business for yourself or for someone else. If you are not transparent with how the money is allocated your financial forecasts are irrelevant.

Use the simple principle of transparency to increase investment, improve relationships with customers and suppliers, and create an overall positive reputation. You will also reduce risk of deceit by making it clear that fraudulent activity will be detected and there will be consequences. Speaking of which, the principal that supports transparency is compliance. It can be difficult to be transparent when you are not compliant. Let's look at why it is important to be compliant and how you can bring that into your life.

Compliance

When people hear the word compliance, they think of being heavily regulated and having to meet the demands of these regulations. While there is an element of regulation in the idea of compliance, there is more to it than that. You need to be compliant for the government and your stakeholders, as well as your own sake and for the business. Being compliant will help you and your business more than it will protect or help anyone else.

From the definition, you can already anticipate how compliance will protect you from financial fraud and errors just as much as it protects your stakeholders and the government. I want you to see compliance as a double-edged sword. Having a governing body that regulates how an accounting statement is presented will help to protect your company from fraud and your investors from the false presentation of accounts. It cannot be any other way.

Think about how much you could lose if your employees can manipulate accounts and present whatever they want to you. You could lose money without even knowing it—millions even—depending on how big your business is. On the other hand, you can trick investors into thinking your business is making a lot of money and lure them to invest when in reality your numbers are far below what you show.

Since there is an international standard for businesses to record their accounts, there is a greater chance you will get more accurate data that represents what is happening in your company. Publicly traded companies have to publish their accounts for everyone to see and you can use these to make comparisons. You can trust the results you get are reliable since the companies use the same regulations and accounting standards.

In the case of the government, your accounting reports are critical to demonstrate you are compliant with the rules and regulations. The regulations are designed to help companies make their accounting easier. The government produces a framework for businesses to follow. This framework can help businesses identify and understand the regulations that apply to them, as well as develop and implement procedures to comply with those regulations. Compliance can also help businesses avoid penalties and fines for non-compliance by the government, yet another great positive of compliance.

So how can you bring this to your personal life? Well, this is one of those concepts that mostly apply to big institutions, but there is a way you can use it in your personal life as well. The main idea behind compliance is transparency and accountability. This means that you should be able to use your finances responsibly and be transparent with all transactions.

You can be transparent yourself by not spending your money without accounting for its use properly. Yes, it's possible to hide your spending habits from yourself. Most people cannot account for the bulk of their money by the end of the month, meaning they will use the money and then fail to remember what exactly used all of it.

Unless you have some sort of accounting system you will have a really hard time keeping track of your spending habits. Ask yourself how you used the last paycheck you received. How much of it can you account for? It can be a stunning realization to acknowledge you have no idea where your money goes. Do not worry. This is why you should create and manage a budget, and have some form of accounting system to record everything you do. If you do not account for your money, you will not know where it goes.

In summary, compliance is essential for protecting the company from financial fraud and errors and it helps to ensure that all financial transactions are properly recorded and reported. This prevents fraud by making it more difficult for employees to hide or misrepresent financial information. You can also have this system in your life, making it hard for poor spending habits to go unnoticed.

There you have it. Investing, and finding investors, is not an easy thing to initiate, but once you get your accounts in order, it becomes easier. Investors are attracted to your business initially through the numbers. They desire to make more money which invites them to invest in your business, so your business needs to present accounting statements that accurately depict how well your company is doing.

The investors are protected through the regulations that surround the reporting system. These regulations make sure that you do not overstate your profits to invite investors or downplay your profits to reduce the payouts to the investors. This process makes it easy for you and your company to maintain a transparent system and relationship with your investors.

Now, let's move on to the next chapter and see how the modern world and technology work together to make it easier for you to create and maintain an efficient accounting system.

Chapter 9:

The Impact of Technology on

Accounting

These days you cannot discuss anything without talking about technology. There have been such great advancements in technology over the past decade that it is a crucial part of every operation in business and life. If you are going to understand accounting and use it effectively, you need to understand how it is tangled up in the technology world and how you can unlock its potential through technology.

The fact is, you might already be using technology for accounting and just never thought about it. Do you have a calculator on your phone that you use to calculate prices, conversions, and other money metrics? Maybe you use a budget application of some sort, or you even have a small accounting system running on your device. In some cases, it's just that to-do list that acts as a budget, or that Cash App, PayPal, or banking application that you have installed.

All of these items represent the interaction of accounting and technology. You should know how to use each one appropriately and effectively. This chapter will investigate how technology has helped to shape the accounting world, and how you can use it to simplify and increase accuracy in your own financial life. Regardless of whether you use accounting for your small business or your personal life you will need to incorporate technology. You will be introduced to some of the applications you need to have to manage your business and life the right way.

Automation of Routine Tasks

Accounting has made it easy to process transactions in an orderly way and technology has made that process even easier. Where you would have had to enter transactions one by one, you can let the accounting system automatically take care of some of the processes through the automation of routine tasks. You already have this happening in one way or another in your business or life. If you have any payments that go through your bank monthly without needing you to reinitiate them every time, that is an example of how technology makes it easy for you to manage your money.

Many of your subscriptions might already be on an automated system of some sort so that they go through without you needing to be involved every single time. Most of the financial transactions in the world right now have been automated to some extent and we can only imagine that it is going to happen more and more as technology advances. Later. we will talk about how you can and should stay in touch with the ever-transforming and growing accounting systems in a world where it feels hard to keep up with the technological changes.

I want you to now take some time to create your automated system that can make your life slightly easier. I want you to start by listing the main expenses you have for your business or your personal life. Use your journal and take your time. Think of the expenses that may be the most stressful, especially rent, mortgage payments, or loans. Write down as many of these as you can in a list and then when you are done, we will go through them one on one and try to figure out how we can control them to create the automated accounting system for your business and your life.

Before we move on to creating this automated system, you will also need to make a list of all your income sources with the amounts you receive on average every week or month. If the amount varies, I want you to choose the lower end, an amount that you know you will always be able to make. Now, I know, there are so many things that could happen that you have not planned for that can change this income stream. Consider a plan to manage any sudden change to ensure you meet your regular financial obligations. While this plan would not be entirely foolproof, it is a very good place for you to start.

Let's go back to the list that we made earlier and I now want you to look at the expenses and mark the ones that repeat in certain intervals. Things like your heat and water bills, your rentals, and food would fall under this category. For your business, this might be the materials you need every month or the labor you have to pay including any other services you hire to fulfill your obligations.

After you have picked the expenses you have to pay regularly, I want you to see which of these you can pay through a recurring automated payment facilitated by your bank. This is a way for you to make payments every month without having to process the transactions every time. In addition to this, I want you to also have only two days where you pay all of these expenses including the ones that cannot be included in automatic payments.

Think of it this way, if you pay off all of these expenses in two consecutive days, you will not have to think about doing it for the rest of the month. If you pay them on different dates scattered throughout the month, then there will always be some big payments that make you feel anxious. You need to create a predictable and intentional plan for your payments, one that will help you to stress less about the payment dates and time frames.

Data Analysis Tools for Better Insights

You can also use digital tools to analyze your accounts and have the reports generated for you. It will be more appropriate to use this when you still have a small business or when you are only managing your accounts. The bigger and more complex the business gets, the harder it is for you to use digital tools to prepare an analysis of your transactions.

I would advise you to use the digital tools from the start so that the data is already loaded into the system as you go through the week and enter your transactions. Using such tools can be very helpful when you are only a beginner as you might not even know where to place which types of transactions otherwise. As we said earlier, the more you practice, the better you will get. Use the accounting concepts of cash flow and profit and loss that we discussed in earlier chapters to guide you. If you start by using a system to analyze and produce reports for your financial transactions then soon you will have also learned to do it by yourself.

I am going to now recommend some tools that you can use both for your small business and your personal life. I will leave out the big and somewhat complex systems so that you get the basics from a system that is accessible and easy to use. The first system I ever used for accounting was Pastel, and I used this with very little prior training. This made me hate using digital systems for accounting, but the more I did it the better I became, and before I knew it, I knew my way around the system. I wish I had started with an easy system. I would have learned much faster that way. At least I can share my lessons learned with you. Accounting is like going up a staircase, as long as you keep taking the next step, and at your own pace, holding on to the rail, then you will safely get to the end.

Cloud-Based Software Solutions

Cloud-based software is improving and has become one of the technologies we can look forward to seeing more of in the future. When accounting started, everything was being recorded in a physical book that would be read and accessed only if the books were physically there. This brought with it limitations when it came to collaboration and team work as it was very hard to access the information.

After this, we moved to the digital age and we started recording information on computers and storing them locally on servers. This was more efficient as the information could be accessed by more people and was relatively safe compared to only having it in physical books. This is what most people are still using today even though they are quickly moving over to cloud-based accounting.

Cloud-based accounting is done online and everything is captured and stored in real time. There are so many benefits to cloud-based accounting and we will explore most of them in this section. It's important that you understand how accounting is evolving and become a part of that process so that when some tools become obsolete, you will not be stuck. Accounting functions always progress with the times because, in a way, it's part of what drives the change. Think about it. At the center of every advancement, there is investment; money is what people use to create and participate in the economic world as we know it. This means that the ways we understand and present financial knowledge have to move fast so it can facilitate the advancement in the economy.

SAP),

You can then build other tools around that to make the system even more effective. For instance, you can have a system for online signatures and approvals as well and add a way for the teams to communicate as they need to through the platform. The increase in the efficiency of cloud-based solutions is what has led to the rise of remote work. Since the 2020 COVID-19 pandemic, we have witnessed how important it is to have this type of flexibility.

Accounting is finding a place in the online world. There are so many other things that we still need to improve, but we have already got the basics of accounting in most online systems and more are on their way. With its logical roots, accounting practices benefited greatly from this technology. If you can, use a platform that is cloud based for your small business and even for your personal life. You will have the ability to travel and still have visibility to everything happening and you will rest assured knowing your data is not vulnerable to theft and damage. Not to say there is no risk to using the cloud-based systems. There are many cybersecurity threats that can impact your data and systems . However, this is still a far safer and more efficient option than the older methods of accounting.

Technology has had a huge impact on our lives and accounting has not been left out of this movement. Accounting has been at the forefront of the movement of technology and is even the reason we keep pushing the boundaries of technology. The fact that people need to have secure but easy ways of sending and receiving money has led to the developments that monitor and advance our financial sector now.

Your phone and laptop are an extension of who you are and they are here to make your life easier. They can also make your accounting journey easier and more fun and that is not something you should pass on. It's okay to start with the simple accounting system before you move on to major systems, the most important thing is for you to start learning and eventually, you will be able to use any accounting system you want.

With this wealth of information, we are ready to proceed and discuss Small Businesses and Accounting. Remember, the main reason anyone should seek to learn accounting should be to improve their own life and find a way to understand and represent the financial transactions in their life. In this upcoming chapter, we will go over the most important parts of personal accounting.

Chapter 10:

Accounting for Small Business

Management

Close to 99% of all businesses in the United States of America are small businesses (Main, 2022). This is because most people are realizing that they have unique skills and advantages that allow them to provide products and services that will help the world. The introduction of commerce online has made it easy for people to market and sell their products and services without needing to have a huge budget first.

The development of social media has allowed companies to reach the desired audiences by creating and pushing content online while the ecommerce platforms like Shopify and Amazon have made it very easy for companies to both ship their products and receive payments for them. All this has created a diverse and rich community online where you can also develop your small business, doing what you love and giving people what they want while making money.

However, one area that is not as easy to understand and incorporate into your small business is accounting. While accounting is a background function that most people will not even hear about, it is a vital part of any business, especially if the business wants to make a profit and continue to grow. In this chapter, I will tell you everything you need to know to be able to establish and maintain an accounting system that works for your business.

I want you to use your journal again and jot down notes as we go through these sections. Remember, the more you are involved in the process, the more suitable it will be for your business. The information I will be providing here will only assist with outlines for how to create the accounting system you need for your business. You will need to pick up the pieces and create a system that works for you. The success of your business is in the hands of your financial management and that lies in your ability to understand and use the appropriate accounting systems.

Business Valuation

The most important thing when you start a small business is to evaluate your business financially and know what it is worth. This is the basis for scaling your business and determining how much the equity you get will be worth. Business valuation is the process of deciding what your venture is worth so that you can base the rest of your accounting processes on that.

In a previous chapter, we went over the balance sheet and how it represents the assets, liabilities, and equity. These components should be determined from the start. One of the mistakes people make when they start a business is that they do not record their transactions from the start. By failing to do this, you also fail to correctly determine the value of the capital you have invested in the company.

Let's walk through the elements of the evaluation that you need to recognize as you start your small business. If you do not start your business on the right note, then you might have a hard time understanding where your finances are going later. This is a very practical session and I want you to try and apply these principles and ideas to your business as you go through them. We are going to look at the full business evaluation process so that you understand the value of your business and then we will move on to bookkeeping and other elements.

While there is a lot that goes into determining the value of a business, there are six elements that are imperative and should not be missed. The first of these elements is the revenue generated by the business. As we have covered already, revenue is the amount your business makes from its core activities. While this figure alone does not give the complete picture, it shows how big your business is and the potential growth as well.

Imagine you meet two people and they both want you to invest in their business. One says they have a business that is making $120,000 in revenue every month and the other says they are making more than a million in revenue each month. Based on this information, which of the two are you more likely to invest in? Yes, the one with the bigger revenue numbers. This is one of the many ways you can evaluate and present your small business to potential customers and investors.

The next element adds a bit of context to the first measure and helps you as the owner to understand the value of your business more. I want you to imagine, that you have an option to own one of the two businesses we went over in the first point; business A, which has $120,000 in revenue, and business V which has over one million in revenue. However, now you also know that company A has expenses of $20,000 per year while company V has $950,000 in expenses each year.

This completely changes everything, as it shows the profit and efficiency of the businesses. You always want to use the least amount of resources to create the most wealth and sometimes you can make a lot of money but at such a high cost that it does not make significant profits.

The next component you need to consider and record as you continue with the evaluations is the assets the business has. Assets are items that are valuable and that can be turned into cash when a business closes. If a business has more assets, then they are worth more and they can use this to get more investment, as the assets are often seen as positive. If a business has only $5,000 in assets and you invest $10,000 as a loan, should the business close down, it might fail to pay you back the full amount of your investment as there isn't enough value in the assets to cover the amount.

It's important to know which items you should record as your assets and how to record them. You can refer back to the earlier chapters for guidance on this where we talked about the balance sheet and how to prepare it.

Fourth, the debts and credits that are attributed to the business are also a part of the business's value. Even though this is both money the business has not paid out and money it has yet to receive, it can have a huge impact on whether the business continues or not. If your business owes many suppliers money and it gets to a point where it can no longer pay those suppliers, then the business will have to declare bankruptcy and be liquidated. It's important to keep a healthy balance between the debts and the credits of the business so that you avoid losing the business to the debts.

While all the other elements we have gone over are direct values that can be calculated and easily quantified, not all elements of evaluating a business are like that. Goodwill refers to the reputation, culture, and reliability of the business and the value that it brings to your business. Imagine you are running a business that is known for high-quality products and for always making deliveries on time. The reputation of the company can be difficult to assess and cannot be quantified easily either, but it is an advantage that the company would have over its competitors.

You need to note everything that gives your company an edge over the competition and record that as part of the value of your company. Such things can include where the company is located, the customers, the work culture that attracts employees, and anything else that gives the company a good public image.

After looking at these aspects, we will also look at the risks that the business is facing. Such risks will negatively affect your business and reduce its value even though they may not be recognized. Think of a company that is in the distribution business and that transports fish from a lake 200 miles away to sell to a market in a small town. Most of the butchers will probably buy the meat from this company making up a huge part of its market. Now, imagine a situation where the government says they are looking at the conservation of fish across the country and they are going to limit—and maybe completely ban—fishing in certain parts of the country. Because of this uncertainty, the company could lose some of its value because it is at risk of losing its source product.

With how fast the advances in technology are these days, there are many businesses that are closing as they have failed to adapt to the changes brought by technology. I want you to look at your business and consider how secure it is from becoming obsolete due to advancements in technology. Use your journal to record what you think are the biggest risks to your business and how you can avert them or reduce how much the risks can affect you. The very ability to have risk aversion schemes in place will help to increase the value of your business.

Once you have considered all of these factors, you can use this data to come up with an estimated value for your company. You can have an accountant consultant look at the data and give some input on what the value of the business is or you can do this all by yourself by using the balance sheet format that we went through earlier in the book.

You can use this data to make decisions about your business including how to value your shares and how to expand your business. You must understand the value of your business before you attempt to sell any of your shares or any other type of equity. The most common use of evaluations is to determine how much your business is worth. Regardless of whether you want to sell it or not, you should always have an evaluation of your business with you.

Bookkeeping

After you have determined the value of the business and know what you are working with, the next thing is to create a bookkeeping practice that will work for your business. Bookkeeping is the process of recording the transactions of the company systematically and securely treating and storing the data collected. Prior to the onset of technology, accountants would record everything that happened in the business in a book or in a collection of books that they kept with them. This is where the name bookkeeping came from. The bookkeeper would manage and maintain the books that contained the financial transactions of the company.

I think it is important to think of bookkeeping in that way even though we do not have to write everything down like they did previously. The main idea is that you need to think like a bookkeeper and use that to create records that guide your accounting now. As for yourself, is everything that happens in the business being recorded somewhere?

If transactions are being recorded, then are they being recorded accurately and completely? A good record would show the day when the transaction took place, the source of the money, where it went, and the value exchanged. After that, you need to ask yourself where you are keeping the books and if that is a safe option for information that important. With the basics in place, you can then go into the details of how the transactions are treated in the different ledgers and accounts that the company has.

A good accounting system will provide a clear and concise overview of your financial performance accurately and on time. This will also include the ability to access the reports whenever necessary for decision-making. Your accounting system must be easy to track, organize, and audit whenever it is necessary to do so. It's important to note that the accounting system is not only the software that you use to record and process transactions, it is more than that. It includes all the connections between the users, software, hardware, and physical transactions taking place. Everything that feeds into the accounting process is part of the system, including the data, rules and regulations, and management reports.

Cash Flow Management

Business is all about money. Money is used to create value that can make even more money. The clients are willing to exchange money for goods and services and every other stakeholder is also connected to the business based on money in one way or another. The suppliers want to get money for their services and products. The employees want money for their labor, and the investors want profit from their investments. Given this is how businesses run, if you are going to run one successfully, you need to understand how money moves in your small business.

Every transaction has one of three things happening; either you are losing money, you are making money, or you are converting money into another form. Let's go through an exercise for a moment. I am going to write down seven transactions, and I want you to use your journal to record whether you think they are losing money, making money, or converting money to another form.

1. You buy a new machine for your T-shirt printing business for $989.99.

2. You pay your electrical bill.

3. You receive an amount of $450 as a prepayment for the work contracted.

4. You have just bought yourself a car from the business profits as a bonus for all the good work you are doing.

5. You have just paid your rentals for the month.

6. You have just deposited $688 into your personal bank account as payment for all your labor throughout the month.

7. You have just received a huge discount from a supplier who failed to fulfill the order on time.

What do you think are the implications of these transactions on how your money is moving? I want you to think of this scenario from the perspective of the business and as an individual, what do you think happened to the business with each of these transactions?

Cashflow is very important and should be seriously considered every day if you are to run the business successfully. While the business might have a lot of money, it might not have the liquidity to use all of that money all the time. Because of this, you can employ proper cash flow management to make sure that you always have enough cash on hand to pay for your expenses and obligations on time.

Financial Projections

The fourth and final element in managing your small business is making accurate financial projections and using them to make good decisions for your business. The main idea of accounting for a small business, is for you, the owner, to have visibility and know what is happening financially in your business. You should use this as a method to open your mind and understand what is happening in your business each day. The more you understand the value of your business, record the transactions accurately, and use all the data to make predictions for your business, the more you are likely to succeed.

Financial projections are important because if you know where you are going, you can prepare now to get there faster and more efficiently. If, through the reviews, you realize that you are going to have a problem with cash in the future, you can combat the problem now and stop it from ever happening. If on the other hand, you realize that there is an opportunity for growth ahead, you can capitalize on it and make the best of the opportunity.

Financial projections are done using tools that make it easy for you and your team to track and manage the future of your business through well-organized planning. You will have to build a systematic process that simplifies business tasks such as planning, budgeting, and forecasting, which are the elements of financial projections.

Budgeting

Budgeting for small businesses is done by planning out the fixed costs for the business into the future and then adding the variable using the most relevant and likely values. After you have done this, you will not need to make sure that you have enough money to cover all of the costs. Remember what we covered about cash flow? You might have enough assets to pay for all the expenses, but it will need to be converted to cash otherwise you can fail to pay on time.

After determining what you need to pay, when you need to pay it, and where you will get the money, you need to automate the process. Make it such that you do not have to think about the payments consistently, but you will have both a date and an assured source of funds taking away the stress of planning for payments as they come up. Budgeting is a process that is meant to take away the stress of choosing how to spend the business's money, giving you a chance to schedule payments regularly and leaving the rest of the time for you to be productive and focus on the bottom line.

The ability to estimate future revenue and additional income will also help you and your team forecast how the resources will be used. You need to stay ahead of the curve and plan for everything before it happens. If you do not do this, you could miss out on so many opportunities and you might even lose money.

Starting a business can be very demanding and stressful, especially if you do not know how to record, present, and understand your financial statements. This is not a minor inconvenience to a small business as everything revolves around making money and minimizing costs. The truth is, you will need to know almost all the sides of accounting when you are running a small business and cannot afford to hire an accountant yet.

You will need to understand how to set up the accounting statements, and also how to prepare the management accounts data that will then inform your decisions. On top of this, you will have to pay tax for the business along with meeting other statutory obligations. This will not always be easy, but it can be done with some training, most of which you have already had an introduction to through this book.

You should keep learning and improving your accounting skills so that it takes you less time to manage and you have more time to promote your business. In the next chapter, we are going to look at how the trends in accounting are changing with time and how you need to change and improve your methods as well.

The trends in the development of accounting provide an opportunity for you to create an accounting system that is efficient and secure for your business. That is an opportunity you should take full advantage of. Let's move on and see how you can future-proof accounting for your small business.

Accounting for Personal Finance Management

Now I want us to look at some elements of accounting that are both applicable to the small business environment and that you can also use in your personal life. Personal finance is not easy. It often feels like you are policing yourself and that is something we have never been good at as humans. But what would happen if you stopped leaving your finances to chance and took charge of your money? Well, you will not have to wonder for long. I want you to use your journal and record ideas as you implement the concepts that we are going to go through in this section.

If you are going to practice only one of the things in this book, let it be what we are about to go over now. I always like to say that you are an accountant in your own life before you can account for someone else. If you cannot be honest with yourself and look at what you want to do with your money and stick to it, then you will have a hard time making a good accountant.

While we will not in any way exhaust the accounting principles that will help you in your life, we will cover enough to give you a good basis for what financial planning and tracking are. Let's dive right in and look at how you can start to improve your financial health today.

Budgeting

Money can often act like it has a mind of its own sometimes. You can have plans for how you want to use your money, but things never seem to go according to your plans. Pay- check to paycheck and payment after payment, you are always struggling to get your money to do what it actually should; grow. The good thing is there is a way to start having it work for you instead of having to detect what you should use it for.

Let's pretend for a moment that you can tell money exactly what you want it to do and it would do it, how would that change your life? What would you command your money to do for you if you could? Well, the good thing is that you actually can. Through budgeting, you can make sure your finances end up doing what you want them to do and not go to random wants that are not needed.

A budget is your direction to your finances telling them what you want them to do for you during a specific period. The main problem is most people look at budgets as restraints. While there is an element of truth in this, it is not the best way to look at or treat your budget. It is the mindset you create around your budget that makes it work best.

So instead of seeing the budgets as restraints, ask yourself what you could do with the money that would leave you happy and financially secure at the end of the month. You are going to use your money anyway, why not use it for the items that benefit you? In your budget, start by asking yourself what payments you should make during the period. This will be a list of all the obligations you have, like your rentals, bills, and everything else in between. Once you have these listed, you have a good idea of what you need to pay first, and then move on to everything else.

Think about who you are and what you need to get done that month. You should use your money to make yourself and your life better, so it would help to know what you need for your personal life if you are going to make the budget that will help you reach those goals. I want you to try making a budget for this month in your journal and follow it as closely as you can. The more specific your budget is the better you will be at managing your resources. Budgeting is the most important part of personal finance, so now let's look at other elements that can help to improve your financial health as well.

Tracking Expenses

Most people mix up tracking their expenses with making a budget and this can often make both less effective. A budget is supposed to tell your money what it is supposed to do for you while the expense tracker will then show how you used your money. Just because you directed your money towards certain expenses, it does not mean that it will go that way, and because of this, you need to be able to track how your money ends up working through the period.

I advise you to use the tracking tools to adjust your budget for the next period, especially if there are impending costs that will be realized. The idea is that you should follow your budget such that your expense tracker runs parallel to your budget. The best part is—with the rise of technology—there are now a couple of applications that make it easy for you to do both budgeting and tracking your expenses.

Creating a budget and tracking your expenses is very important and it can be the difference between failing to maintain and manage your finances, and being in total control. Let's look at how the future will help to shape the world of accounting as we know it, and what your part in all of this will be.

Chapter 11:

Future Trends in Accounting

Let's talk about where the world of accounting is heading and how you can position yourself to be a part of the transformation. As you have seen, most of the transformation that has led us to this point with accounting has all been because of a need coupled with the advancement of technology. Well, we still have the need, and technology is expanding. This means you need to be positioned to understand how the world of accounting is going to transform in the coming years and learn to incorporate those changes into your life.

The biggest leap in technology right now is on the Artificial Intelligence (AI) front, and there has been no exception for accounting. Through various new concepts, the idea of what accounting is and how it works is changing drastically and beckoning for you to grow and change as well. You have a part to play in all of this. You are both the person who should be positioned to get the most out of these systems and also the person who could potentially influence how AI interacts with the accounting process.

As I mentioned before, the more technology advances, the more personal and customizable the accounting system gets. This is great for someone like you. Now you do not need to know as much about the intricacies of accounting. You do need to know the components and principles of accounting that apply to your needs. You can have a more customizable accounting experience now more than ever and that is the great gift of technology. Through this chapter, we are going to explore how you can understand the latest trends in accounting and the impacts of these advancements on the business world. The areas that we will focus on are AI, machine learning, blockchain technology, and cyber security. These are the main issues with the advancement of accounting onto the online platform.

Artificial Intelligence (AI)

There has not been a more trending topic online in recent years than Artificial intelligence (AI). AI has been used for almost everything of late, from creating content online to helping people with creative output, etc.

In accounting, it is not that easy; however, there are so many requirements from the accounting community that make it very hard to use AI. The best we can do at the moment is to use AI to take care of repetitive tasks and automate the recording and processing of some accounts. AI can also be used to prepare the outputs, such as the financial and management reporting. However, you will most certainly need an accountant to use the AI so that you can get the desired results. Also, because of all the regulations and restraints of the preparation of accounting, you still need humans to check the work, approve it, and explain what the final reports mean.

This is not to say AI does not have a place in accounting. We are already seeing AI being used to take over several accounting processes. AI is rapidly changing the world of accounting through AI-powered tools that are being used to automate data entry, audit, and tax preparation. AI is also being used to develop new insights from financial data.

Since AI can process more data compared to humans in a given time period, by teaching the AI to go through multiple data collections, you can have it analyze and simplify the data for the accountants. Imagine you are an accountant and you want to analyze the amount of sales made every week for a whole year. With AI, you can use a program that can instantly pull all of that data together and produce graphs that show exactly what you want.

The trick is, that you need to know what you are looking for in the data. AI is only a tool that can give the accountants the resource to do what they need to do faster and more effectively. In the case of auditing, the AI can point out areas that do not add up or where certain descriptions seem off. It is up to the auditor to verify and try to figure out where the error is. This being said, we can determine that the role of the auditor will expand to verify the the programming behind the AI used to produce the data, as well as validating the data itself.

Efficiency

The biggest benefit of AI is increased efficiency which leads to many of the other benefits. While humans are very good at things like analysis and logic, they are more prone to making errors when working with huge amounts of data. This is where AI comes in. If you had an Excel report with thousands of transactions and asked AI to pick out certain elements, it would be able to do it virtually instantaneously.

This benefit from technology is not a new one. Excel and other programs like it have been providing tools that allow humans to process huge amounts of data more accurately. AI works between these tools and the end user, and makes it easy for the end user to interpret the information with a limited learning curve. Imagine the difference between using formulas through Excel to extract and add up certain elements, and just asking the program to do it. Anyone can instruct AI to present all sales totals for every week for the past year without the need to understand the program, but with older programs, you would have to use instructions, such as macros, specific to the program to get the data.

AI has made it easier to interact with accounting languages in ways that no one imagined. and it is going to get even better in time. Another benefit of AI that is often overlooked is how it helps to reduce costs. With big corporations that require bigger and more secure systems for accounting, the initial investment is significant and will often make it seem like integrating AI into the accounting systems is expensive. However, when you consider the amount of time you are going to save in the long run, AI is the most cost-effective option.

AI will also help to reduce costs by reducing the labor hours and personnel needed to input data and maintain the company's accounts. There is no denying that AI is still far from completely replacing humans in the accounting field as its main job is still processing commands given by the accountant. However, a company will use the other accountants they have either in other departments as auditors or on contract, which would certainly affect resource consumption and final costs of operations.

In addition to processing data faster and more accurately, AI will also help accountants prepare a variety of reports as there is more processing power to run different types of reports at once. To help management make better decisions, one of the things that the accountants can do is provide more variations for the performance reports and more detailed interpretation of the other financial reports.

AI can isolate data and help the accountant filter out information and get very specific reports to deal with key areas of the business. Imagine a situation where a report shows all the purchases made and when they were made for one of the branches of the company. What if the managers want to discuss whether customers bought the products using cash, swipe, and in which currency? Through the use of AI, the accounting team can isolate these elements faster and produce the results more quickly than they would have been able to otherwise.

AI is also intuitive enough to pick out the probability of error in reports after you run them. Imagine you have just prepared a simple rundown of all the cash you have made in the past two months. By programming your AI, you can have it remind you of some principles that can affect your report's accuracy depending on the purpose of use. One of the things it can highlight is if one of the payments was made for goods you had sold five months ago. According to the matching principle, this amount would have to have been recorded five months ago since that is when the sale was made and not in the past two months. Such errors often go unnoticed with accounting reports but the introduction of artificial intelligence may be the best solution.

However, there are some challenges that you will still meet even when you are using AI. You will also have new challenges that were not there before because you are using AI. The main issue you will have to contend with the moment you start to incorporate AI is the possibility of cyber attacks.

AI has to be hosted somewhere, and it is not always the safest option. For it to work, in the majority of cases, the AI gets access to your data and moves it from the secure system it is hosted in to process it and then bring back the results. Because all of this happens in the background, it might be really hard for you to see how vulnerable the data is and that is what makes it even more dangerous.

Another problem with AI is that is only as good as the data it has been given to work with and it will only produce as much as it has been programmed to. This is often a problem because AI gives the impression that it is working logically to come up with reports and improve the quality of the data. This is not true; however, as what it is doing is just executing the programs that it has been given using the data it has been provided. So AI cannot improve the quality of the data or come up with new and novel reports unless it has been programmed to do so.

Currently, there is a big debate on ethical considerations when it comes to using AI across the board. AI systems can be used to make decisions that have ethical implications for the societies in which they are used. This fact, coupled with the need for accounting to adhere to the regulations, means you will need a lot of human intervention to make sure that the process is as compliant and ethical as possible. This is where the auditing function is a necessity.

Overall, AI has the potential to revolutionize the accounting profession, especially in the coming years. We still need to carefully consider the challenges associated with AI before adopting it completely and come up with plans to avert any risk that might come your way. AI-powered tools and software are already being adopted into so many different parts of the commercial world, and the results have been phenomenal. From tax preparation, and data entry, all the way to audit, AI is a blessing to the accounting world.

Machine Learning (ML)

Machine learning and blockchain technologies have energized the backbone of the surge in technological advances over the past few years. Their presence has the potential to completely change and transform the accounting profession for good. "Machine learning is a branch of artificial intelligence (AI) and computer science which focuses on the use of data and algorithms to imitate the way that humans learn, gradually improving its accuracy."(IBM, 2023)

The accounting world can expect to see a significant improvement in the way systems capture and enter data, audit, and prepare taxes based on how they incorporate machine learning into accounting programs. In addition to these functions being improved, we will also have better efficiency in all operational areas of the business. For example, machine learning can automate inventory control and product tracking to increase security and reduce stock audit costs. In some cases, you can even use machine learning and technology to track your products as they weave their way through the distribution channels to the customers and also track the raw materials as they come to you.

You can be assured that both machine learning and blockchain are going to be revolutionary to the accounting process. You can also be assured that there are challenges that the accounting systems have to be aware of, especially since the technology for machine learning and blockchain is still in its developmental stages.

One of the main challenges that has already begun to emerge is how the systems use, process, and keep the confidential data of the company secure. The security systems for the hardware and software that run these programs have not yet been mastered, leaving some serious instances of data breaching in the past few years. Some major companies like Sony have been victims of these hacks and we can expect that more of this will happen before we finally have tight and hacking-proof systems to protect the accounting systems (Reed, 2023).

Even if the data does not get hacked or improperly managed through the system, there is a very high possibility that the systems will still struggle to produce the reports they should be free of error. Machine learning happens when algorithms use masses of quality data to train themselves and learn the components in the data. this is a problem for machine learning in accounting as it is first off really hard to get high-quality and comprehensive data that is not confidential.

This means most of the training for machine learning has been completely done on simulation data and this does not prepare it well to handle the real diversity of accounting data. Machines find it easier to analyze and create parts out of data that have some form of order to it. Accounting data may have limited or no order or format to it depending on the quality of its source. This makes it hard for the machines to use the data or to use it accurately when they do.

So, in a nutshell, machine learning algorithms are not yet sophisticated enough to run accounting systems alone reliably. Accounting makes decisions that impact the lives of people and the economy as a whole and this means the stakes are very high, requiring all companies to be as ethical and compliant as possible. With machines, it can be very hard to judge how ethical and fair the decisions are when they are produced.

Cybersecurity Challenges

As we have been moving more and more towards work online, we have also been facing new threats in accounting. The biggest of these are cyber threats which leave the company accounting information at risk of being accessed by unauthorized personnel. Cyber threats and hacker attacks are becoming more and more dangerous having risen significantly in the past few years.

This has led to the rise of cybersecurity systems in accounting whose main purpose is to protect the company's accounting information and systems from unauthorized access, use, disclosure, disruption, modification, or destruction. Accounting firms need to have strong cybersecurity measures in place to protect their client's financial information, just as the clients themselves implement measures to make sure the accounting information remains safe.

Accounting data often includes personal details for the employees and other details that are private and confidential. Imagine how dangerous it would be if the payroll information got out and people were able to not only see how much the employees received, but their social security numbers, addresses, and their banking details. Because of things like this, all financial and accounting systems require special and impeachable protection. It is not just protection for now that is needed, as technology has been getting better, so have the tools for hacking, therefore, the security systems need to be constantly updated to make sure that they are secure against the latest hacking systems.

Many areas of the accounting function need to be secured, but we will look at the big four which include data security, network security, cybersecurity awareness training, and incident response planning. Let's go over them in detail and see what each of these means.

Data Security

All the company's information must be stored responsibly and used appropriately. This is the first step to creating cybersecurity for your company's accounting data because if the data is easy to access, then it will be very hard to protect. There should be clear guidelines on who can access what type of data, when, and for what reason. If this hierarchy is not created, then even the employees will have access to the data even when they do not.

Giving access to employees when it is not necessary will lead to the stealing of data and fraud among other things. The company should always know who accessed the data, how, and where so that if anything goes wrong, they can always trace their steps back and find out where they went wrong. At the end of the day, data security is all about making sure that accounting data is protected from unauthorized access, use, disclosure, disruption, modification, or destruction.

Network Security

Network security is the practice of protecting computer networks from unauthorized access, use, disclosure, disruption, modification, or destruction. It includes a wide range of security measures, such as firewalls, intrusion detection systems, and data encryption. In the given context, network security is important to protect the confidentiality, integrity, and availability of data and systems.

Cybersecurity Awareness Training

The systems within an organization are used by people, and this means no matter how secure you make the systems, you will also need to get the people responsible for the systems to be on board with your fight against cyber attacks, or else they become the weakness that the hackers will use. To get the employees on board, you need to create programs to teach them about the dangers of cybersecurity compromise and how they can make sure they do not create gaps in the system

The first thing you will want to train the employees on is finding, identifying, and avoiding phishing scams. Phishing scams are emails or websites that try to trick people into giving away their personal information, such as passwords or credit card numbers and they often send emails with deceiving links to bait your employees into connecting with them. If you teach your employees how to identify phishing scams, you can reduce the likelihood of them being baited through emails, which is a big relief as this is the most popular form of communication at work.

Following this, you need to make sure that every employee is using a strong private password and two-factor authentication whenever possible as long as they are accessing company systems on the device. Strong passwords are difficult to guess, and two-factor authentication adds an extra layer of security by requiring users to enter a code from their device in addition to their password. Passwords should be unique and changed regularly as well. You need to make these security measures a requirement for all the employees at the company.

After you have educated the employees on how they can keep their devices secure, you need to make sure the devices are all up to date, especially with security certificates and software updates. Most updates come with new security patches that will greatly improve the security levels of the device and systems hosted on it. Where possible the company should make sure they update all of the devices on time, but it should be up to every individual to make sure their device is always up to date.

Being aware of social engineering attacks. Social engineering attacks are attempts to trick people into giving away their personal information or clicking on malicious links. By teaching people how to identify social engineering attacks, you can help them avoid becoming victims of these attacks.

Cyber threats are always evolving, every month there is something new with its way of trying to get into your system and steal your data. Because of this, the company should have and standing IT team that is constantly looking out for new threats and working around the clock to make sure the systems and security of the company network remain safe against cyber threats. The best way to achieve this is by teaching the employees to even check for threats and stay informed for themselves.

Cybersecurity training is important for everyone, but it is especially important for employees that handle sensitive data, like accountants and accounting firms. This is because these employees are often the targets of cyber attacks, and they need to be aware of the latest threats and how to protect themselves. Because of their access to the financial data, accountants may also be the first to identify that an attack is imminent, In the case of accounting, the threat can cost a company significant amounts of money.

Incident Response Planning

Even though you plan to the best of your abilities to secure the company, its systems, and its employees, you will not be able to completely guard against incidents happening. This is why it is important to have a plan of action in case something happens and an attack is identified. Every employee should know what to do if they think there has been an attack, starting with who to tell and what information to provide.

The perfect plan will depend on your organization and how you run it but I will give you some general guidelines on how you can develop the plan from the ground up, highlighting the ideas that are the most important.

There are three questions every employee needs to ask when they have been—or think that they have been—hacked. The first consideration and most important question is, do I have any important information on the hacker and incident? The first step to managing a cyber breach is to get as much information as possible from the employee. You will need to know how the hacker reached out if they did, what time it was, what website it was, and anything else that can help the authorities to identify and catch the hacker.

The second question you need to consider is, have you reported on time and to the right people after taking away access from the threat? As soon as you notice something fishy on your device, you need to cut all connections that might allow the cyber threat to continue. This should be done after you have collected as much information as possible about what is going on.

The final question you need to consider is, have I done enough to stop this from happening again? You should use every attack as an opportunity to guard yourself from having that happen again. The best thing you can do for your company and yourself is make sure that the breach does not happen again by doing everything you can to avoid it.

Here is a brief rundown of things you can do to protect yourself and your company from cyber attacks:

1. Use strong passwords and change them regularly.

2. Be careful about what information you share online.

3. Keep your software up-to-date, including all software and hardware patches.

4. Be aware of the cybersecurity challenges you and your business could face.

5. Know which steps to take to reduce the risk of attack.

6. Know how to act in the event of an attack.

You need to know how to read the current trends and understand how they will affect the way you manage your money in the future. If you do not get a good grasp of these concepts now, you will struggle to catch on later and this can cost you a lot of time, energy, and money. Later may be too late. Accounting is supposed to help you plan and manage your finances in the most hassle-free way possible. That's the goal.

If you understand how to secure your finances and keep your money safe, you can save yourself a lot of headaches in the future. Money management is not only about knowing how to use your money well but also how to keep your money safe. As technology grows the risk of getting your money stolen or compromising your investments through cyber attacks increases, but so do the tools you need to protect your money.

Determine how you can customize a solution for the needs that you have and use that to lead yourself into a more secure future. You do not need to be an accounting guru to do any of this. You only need to be concerned and intentional when it comes to financial management and that drive will help you to understand and keep up with the trends that will affect your finances.

I have a small challenge for you. I want you to take your journal and ask yourself what the most important things are when it comes to your accounting needs. Make a list of all the concerns that you have and then I want you to match them to all the trends that we just discussed. In a journaling session, I want you to think about how you can focus your efforts on learning the ideas and the trends that will help you with your specific pain points.

A great way to do this is to write down what comes into your mind and then go back later and look at which ideas stand out for you. It's always important to know what you expect from your accounting system before you try to build or adapt one. You might have already seen from what we have gone through, that there is so much to accounting and you can never exhaust the utility of the subject. The best you can ever do is find the best practices for your use case and make the best of it. I want you to think hard about this and then when you are comfortable, make a decision and start expanding your knowledge in accounting, thus future-proofing yourself and your business.

Conclusion

There is at least one lesson that I hope you learned as you went through the book. I believe it's such a core idea to accounting, and understanding it will make you a great accountant or a wise user of the system. I hope you learned that accounting—with all its branches and disciplines—is not something to be feared.

How many new ideas did we go over in the book? Well, a lot. There are so many other concepts and ideas in accounting that we did not even cover in this book. Accounting is a system of organizing and managing our finances in a way that makes it easy to see the story of our financial lives.

This means there is no end to accounting. There is so much going on in the world of accounting; so much such that no one is ever an expert. You went through this thinking you were naive and barely know anything about accounting, hoping you would know what accounting was by the end. But that does not happen. No one ever fully understands accounting. That is not the purpose of accounting; you are never meant to understand it fully, you are meant to use it properly to make your life easier. This is where your focus should always be, creating a system that works for you and that will give you an easy and accurate management system for your life, business, and maybe even through your work.

While formal in many ways, the accounting profession is a unique one. The concept of money in and out is standard, the impacts and interpretations are ever-changing. This is not to discourage you from learning accounting. Far from it. As we have progressed on our accounting journey through this book, you have (hopefully) been recording lessons learned in your journal. I encourage you to pick a branch of accounting and investigate it. I know it will add a lot to your life.

References

Accrual principle. (2015). Corporate Finance Institute. https://corporatefinanceinstitute.com/resources/accounting/accrual-principle/

Berry-Johnson, J. (2019). *What is financial accounting? It's critical information.* FreshBooks. https://www.freshbooks.com/hub/accounting/financial-accounting

Carter, T. (2021). *The true failure rate of small businesses.* Entrepreneur. https://www.entrepreneur.com/starting-a-business/the-true-failure-rate-of-small-businesses/361350#:~:text=Only%2020%20percent%20fail%20within

CFI Team. (2023). *Matching principle.* Corporate Finance Institute. https://corporatefinanceinstitute.com/resources/accounting/matching-principle/

Cohen, P. (2021). *Profit and loss statement: Definition, formula, and examples - PRN.* PRN Funding. https://www.prnfunding.com/profit-and-loss-statement-examples#:~:text=Profit%20and%20Loss%20Statement%20Formula

Fernando, J. (2023). *Accounting.* Investopedia. https://www.investopedia.com/terms/a/accounting.asp

Fontinelle, A. (2022). *Introduction to accounting information systems.* Investopedia. https://www.investopedia.com/articles/professionaleducation/11/accounting-information-systems.asp

Grahams, B. (2020). *How to keep your business financial records secure | website design, digital marketing & social media articles, advice, tips and services.* Lobster. https://lobsterdigitalmarketing.co.uk/how-to-keep-your-business-financial-records-secure/

Husain, O. (2023). *14 biggest compliance fines ($1billion and above).* Www.enzuzo.com. https://www.enzuzo.com/blog/biggest-compliance-fines

IBM. (2023). *What is machine learning?* Www.ibm.com; IBM. https://www.ibm.com/topics/machine-learning

Main, K. (2022). *Small business statistics of 2022 – forbes advisor.* Www.forbes.com. https://www.forbes.com/advisor/business/small-business-statistics/

Morris, K. (2022). *Soft skills for accountants: Creative thinking in the workplace.* Www.theaccessgroup.com. https://www.theaccessgroup.com/en-au/blog/act-how-accountants-can-use-creative-thinking-at-work/

NetSuite.com. (2021). *Cost accounting defined: What it is & why it matters.* Oracle NetSuite. https://www.netsuite.com/portal/resource/articles/accounting/cost-accounting.shtml

Publisher, A. removed at request of original. (2016). *12.1 the role of accounting.* Open.lib.umn.edu; University of Minnesota Libraries Publishing edition, 2016. This Edition Adapted from a Work Originally Produced in 2010 by a Publisher Who Has Requested That It Not Receive attribution. https://open.lib.umn.edu/exploringbusiness/chapter/12-1-the-role-of-accounting/#:~:text=Accounting%20is%20a%20system%20for

Reed, C. (2023). *Sony data breaches: Full timeline through 2023.* Firewall Times. https://firewalltimes.com/sony-data-breach-

timeline/#:~:text=September%202023%3A%20Sony%20Inve
stigates%20Alleged

Stanescu, B. (2012). *Top 5: Corporate losses due to hacking.* Hot for Security.
https://www.bitdefender.com/blog/hotforsecurity/top-5-
corporate-losses-due-to-hacking/

Tamplin, T. (2023). *Understanding the definition of accounting & its importance.*
Finance   Strategist.
https://www.financestrategists.com/accounting/introduction-
to-accounting/

What is a balance sheet. (2023). BDC.ca. https://www.bdc.ca/en/articles-
tools/entrepreneur-toolkit/templates-business-
guides/glossary/balance-sheet

What is asset? Definition of asset, asset meaning. (2023). The Economic Times.
https://economictimes.indiatimes.com/definition/asset